THE ASSIST

A Gospel-Centered Guide to Glorifying God through Sports

By

BRIAN SMITH

LUCIDBOOKS

TABLE OF CONTENTS

FOREWORD

First Timothy 4:8 reminds us that "while bodily training is of some value, godliness is of value in every way." Although this is part of a much larger context, Paul's intent is to commend godliness more than demean physical training. Yet his intentional juxtaposition of the two produces a set of interesting questions for the athlete, questions perhaps even more relevant in our cultural moment today than in his own.

What does it mean to be godly in the midst of physical training, and how do we practice it? If we find that athletic training consistently shapes our daily lives, how does faith apply to this physical activity? How do we live consistently at the intersection of physical training and godliness?

In the 1850s, the first American YMCA intentionally sought to mesh evangelical Christianity with the practical pursuit of a sound body, mind, and spirit, equipping young athletes to use sports as a platform for spiritual growth.

One hundred years later, sports ministry organizations such as the Fellowship of Christian Athletes and Athletes in

Action began offering high school and collegiate athletes a vocabulary for faith and sports integration, organizing camps and experiences so athletes and coaches could not only grow personally but also use sports as a platform for ministry.

Given the existence of these organizations and many others like them, struggling with living out the Christian faith in the context of sports is hardly a new concept.

Yet since the beginning of the faith/sports movement, surprisingly little has actually been written in book form to practically help athletes, coaches, and parents think holistically about integrating their Christian faith and their lives as athletes.

People's imaginations regarding faith in sports have often been stunted by pre-game end zone kneeling, mid-game points to heaven after positive plays, and post-game interviews thanking "my Lord and Savior Jesus Christ." Intuitively, people crave more substantive expressions of the Christian faith in the context of sports. They just aren't exactly sure what that should look like. Unfortunately, many athletes become involved in some form of sports ministry without ever thinking deeply about how they are living their own lives, both on the field and off.

The Assist offers just that—an assist to the player, coach, or parent who wants a wide-angled understanding of how to live the Christian faith in the context of sports. Its goal is simple: to move Christians from simply clichéd spiritual sayings decorating their bodies or T-shirts to actually living out their faith in the midst of competition.

Brian Smith takes the canvas of the sports culture and carefully puts color to it, helping us as athletes to practically understand what it looks like to move beyond superficial faith expressions to actually glorifying God—on *his* terms.

Smith writes with the mind of both an athlete and a minister. His words are birthed from years as a Division I track athlete, his long-time service as a campus minister, and literally thousands of conversations with athletes attempting to walk with God in the prime of their athletic lives. He has the practical experience of one who can draw upon his own internal challenges as a competing athlete, combined now with years of being a listener to the struggles of other athletes in his role as a minister. He gets it and has a clear vision of what faith in sports should produce.

The Assist is a biblically driven and practical guide for answering the question, "What does it mean to be a Christian athlete?" While written specifically with the athlete audience in mind, Christian coaches, administrators, and parents will benefit from its teaching. It will also serve as a valuable resource to those in sports ministry, acting as a go-to guide for discussion with athletes and coaches at the high school, collegiate, and professional level.

—Dr. Ed Uszynski

PROLOGUE

The sun was beating down on us in Trinidad, seemingly unsatisfied until every drop of sweat rolled off our backs and onto the track. To call it a track was generous. It was a combination of cement, clay, and dirt wrapped tightly around an abandoned soccer stadium in the middle of nowhere.

My wife and I had just been challenged to an 800-meter track race against a few locals. Having run track in college, specializing in long distance, we were confident we could at least compete without embarrassing ourselves. Ten of us toed the line, and with 100 meters to go, it was just Isaiah and me left in contention. Isaiah was a 16-year-old Trinidad native who had yet to realize his full potential. We rounded the final turn together, but that's as close as I managed to get to him. He found another gear, easily destroying me in the sprint to the finish. While the other runners finished, I peeled myself off the track and found Isaiah sprawled out in the brown grass on the infield.

"Nice work!" I said as I helped him to his feet. "What's the fastest you have ever run an 800?"

"That was my best ever—by 10 seconds," Isaiah said. He seemed genuinely surprised at what he had just accomplished.

We ran two more laps around the track, slowly, as our legs recovered. As we ran, Linsey and I shared with Isaiah that we were missionaries who shared Jesus with athletes. This piqued his interest.

"So you think God cares about sports?" Isaiah asked.

We spent the next five minutes answering this as best as we could in the time we had. That conversation with Isaiah has haunted me ever since. How many others like Isaiah are wondering if God actually cares about what they are doing in the realm of sports and not just spiritual activities? How many athletes could actually give a God-centered, biblical answer for questions like "Does God care about sports, and how can I play my sport in a way that honors him?"

That hot summer day in Trinidad and the conversation that followed became the genesis of this book. After that day, I began to think about the type of resource that could help an athlete like Isaiah compete with a greater purpose in mind. I started to pay attention to how most athletes approached their sport.

What I began to notice unsettled me.

INTRODUCTION

*To think creatively, we must be able to look afresh at
what we normally take for granted.*

—George Kneller

This is a book written from a biblical perspective aimed at helping athletes glorify God in every facet of their sports.

I've noticed a frequent and disturbing disconnect between the words that come out of our mouths as Christian athletes and the actual approach we take to our sports. What frustrates me is that I believe this is not willful rebellion, but ignorance. We lack a clear, biblical understanding of what God wants from us when it comes to competing athletically. That's a problem. If you want to get biblical instruction on how to play your sport and better understand how to connect your role as an athlete with your faith, where do you turn?

So that's the primary reason I've written this book. But it's not the only reason.

I wrote this book because as an athlete you will likely spend anywhere from fifteen to forty hours a week training or competing in your sport. Your dedication to your sport heavily influences your eating, sleeping, and social habits. Add to that how much time you spend thinking about your sport, and you can see that it's a huge part of your life. With all of the time, effort, and energy that go into the world of athletics, we need a resource soaked with theology (proper thinking) and practicality (proper actions) for each circumstance that surfaces within the unique world of sports.

I wrote this book because of what I witnessed in a post-game interview in 2012. The athlete predictably sidestepped the first question and gave the obligatory, "First and foremost, I just want to give all the glory to God." By the third question, he described his sole motivation leading up to the game that week was to make *his* name known to the opposing team and the fans watching. *All the glory to God.* They will remember *my* name. I couldn't believe it.

That is not what really disturbed me, though. I watched that game with fifteen athletes who identify as Christians, yet none of them seemed to catch the hypocrisy on display. They, like most other Christian athletes, had become numb to this spiritual rhetoric. That type of talk and behavior—saying one thing but either not understanding it or, worse, not actually meaning it—has become status quo for the Christian sports culture. I'm saddened by it. But I'm not angry. Christian athletes often make these types of comments because they just don't know any better.

I wrote this book because I've grown tired of the clichéd thinking that dominates the religious sports culture. I'm especially concerned that the word *glory* has turned into a buzzword we flippantly toss around because we've come to believe it's the right answer.

I wrote this book because after asking seventy high-level collegiate Christian athletes about what it means to give glory to

God through their sport, the only answers they could come up with were giving your best effort and giving God all the credit. Athlete, there are so many other ways you can please God through the gift of sports than just those two areas.

I wrote this book because I'm frustrated by the lies athletes believe when it comes to God and their sport.

I wrote this book because we need good, biblical, and practical answers to questions such as these: Does God care about sports? Is it okay for me to want to win? Why would God allow me to get injured? What does it mean to have a platform, and what does God expect me to do with it? What does it even mean to give God glory, and how can I give it to him through a game? Is it okay to pray for success?

This book is for you, the athlete. Not your coach. Not your parents. Not your fans. Athlete, consider this book an assist. From me to you.

My aim in *The Assist* is to reshape the way you think about your sport and present a practical approach to having a gospel-centered perspective for every challenge the world of athletics throws at you.

The first three foundational chapters address what God wants and how athletes should view both God and themselves.

After laying the groundwork, we'll look through the different circumstances brought about by sports and seek to understand how we can glorify God in each of them. We will explore potentially new ways of experiencing, appreciating, and practicing obedience to God in the midst of all the circumstances athletes face—proper motivation, winning, losing, injuries, practice, teammates, gray areas, retirement, and coaches.

Finally, we'll see how the mission and platform afforded to athletes offer a unique opportunity to spread the gospel. With that in mind, we'll give you practical training to leverage your privileged position for the glory of God and the advancement of his kingdom.

We need to learn and execute on making our sport serve us in a way that draws us closer to God. We were created with a longing that cannot be filled by anything or anyone but God. There will always be a ceiling on the amount of happiness earthly things can bring us, and more often than not, we will be disappointed at how low that ceiling is. Ecclesiastes says that God has put eternity in our hearts. The implication is simple: we cannot be satisfied by earthly things. When we use our sport to get more of God, we align ourselves with the way God intended his good gifts, like sports, to work. And in the end, we also get the maximum amount of joy out of it.

> *We need to learn and execute on making our sport serve us in a way that draws us closer to God.*

But what does God get? That's the subject of the first chapter.

CHAPTER 1

ON GLORY

You keep using that word.
I do not think it means what you think it means.

—Inigo Montoya, *The Princess Bride*

A cts 12 has always disturbed me. The Bible tends to
do that sometimes. I think God put in the incident
recounted there—and others like it—to point to a
greater reality. The craziness starts in the first two verses of
the chapter.

"About that time Herod the king laid violent hands on some
who belonged to the church. He killed James the brother of John
with the sword" (Acts 12:1–2).

James was one of Jesus's twelve disciples. It was not some
junior varsity Christian that Herod thrust his sword through.
James was a varsity-level follower of Christ. This story in Acts

tells of the first disciple of Jesus who was martyred. It was a big deal. The baffling part comes a little later, but this first scene sets the context for what follows.

As Acts 12 continues, Herod arrests Peter—another disciple of Jesus. We are left to assume that Herod schemes to have Peter killed as well. But God had a different plan. The night Herod "was about to bring him out" (Acts 12:6), an angel of the Lord helps Peter escape. As Peter reunites with some of the other disciples, we learn that Herod is predictably upset. Verse 19 says that "after Herod searched for him and did not find him, he examined the sentries and ordered that they should be put to death. Then he went down from Judea to Caesarea and spent time there" (Acts 12:19).

Herod has some issues. What comes next in the story leaves me scratching my head. Herod, now in Caesarea, is about to give a speech before the people. The Bible notes that Herod is "angry with the people" (Acts 12:20), which is not shocking at this point in the story as he always seems a little perturbed at something or someone. We learn that Herod puts on royal robes and delivers his passionate speech. Look what happens next.

"And the people were shouting, 'The voice of a god, and not of a man!' Immediately an angel of the Lord struck him down, because he did not give God the glory, and he was eaten by worms and breathed his last" (Acts 12:22–23).

Seriously? Herod kills one of Jesus's chosen twelve. Herod kills the guards who watched Peter. We can probably assume that he has done plenty of other things that the Bible would classify as sin. And yet God takes him out because the crowds are chanting that he has "the voice of a god." God takes him out because he was receiving glory meant for God alone. The Bible says he was taken out *immediately*.

Crowds are shouting his name.

Screaming at the top of their lungs.

Praising him.

Telling him how amazing he is.

Sound familiar, athlete? Let's set aside for a moment what God thinks about sports and answer the bigger question: What does God care about most?

Author and theologian John Piper shines a light on a groundbreaking biblical truth:

> God's ultimate goal is to preserve and display his infinite and awesome greatness and worth, that is, his glory. God has many other goals in what he does. But none of them is more ultimate than this. They are all subordinate. God's overwhelming passion is to exalt the value of his glory. To that end he seeks to display it, to oppose those who belittle it, and to vindicate it from all contempt. It is clearly the uppermost reality in his affections. He loves his glory infinitely.[1]

What God desires most is his glory.

Please do not just take Piper's word for it or my own. Look at what the Bible (God's word) has to say about it.[2]

- Ephesians 1:4–6, 12, 14 – "God chose his people for his glory."
- Isaiah 43:6–7 – "God created us for his glory."
- Jeremiah 13:11 – "Identifies God's purpose for calling Israel: his glory."
- Psalm 106:7–8 – "God rescued Israel from Egypt to make known his power."
- Romans 9:17 – "God's purpose for raising up Pharaoh was to show his power and glorify his name."
- Exodus 14:4, 18 – "God spared Israel in the wilderness for the glory of his name."

- 2 Samuel 7:23 – "The victory God granted for Israel for the glory of his name."
- 2 Kings 19:34 – "Jerusalem was saved for the glory of God's name."
- Ezekiel 36:22–23 – "Israel returned from exile to the glory of his name."
- Habakkuk 2:14 – "One day God will fill the earth with the knowledge of his glory."

Okay, but those were all from the Old Testament. What does the New Testament have to say?

- John 7:18 — "Jesus sought the glory of God in his actions."
- Matthew 5:16 — "Our good works bring glory to God."
- John 14:13 — "God is glorified through our answered prayers."
- John 12:27–28; 17:1 — "Jesus's motivation for enduring suffering was God's glory."
- John 17:24 — "Jesus's desire for us is to see and enjoy his glory."
- 1 Corinthians 10:31 — "Implores us to do everything for God's glory."
- 1 Peter 4:11 — "Instructs us to serve in a way that brings glory to God."

Get the picture? God is infinitely passionate about his glory. You probably already knew that on some level. My guess is, though, that your knowledge was probably based more on cultural norms than biblical conviction. After all, everybody, especially athletes, knows you are *supposed* to "give glory to God."

But what does that mean? If you can't give a clear answer to that question, you need to keep reading. It's time we stop using clichéd Christian phrases when we have no idea what they actually mean.

The Danger in Using Words We Don't Understand

I have a good friend who heard a phrase his freshmen year of college and thought two things:

1. That sounds funny!
2. I am going to start using it.

This friend made this particular phrase a regular part of his vocabulary and spent the better part of his freshmen year using it at practice, parties, Christian events, and in everyday conversation. What was the phrase?

Mofo.

This friend soon found out that it sounded even better when you put the word *crazy* in front of it.

Ignorant as to what this meant, it was not until someone lovingly pulled him aside and informed him what he was actually saying when he called people "crazy mofos" that he finally stopped using it.

While humorous, this friend unintentionally offended many people.

Here's the thing: I think we make a similar error with the word *glory*.

I think very few of us know what glory is and what it looks like to give it to God. My fear is that it has become such a rehearsed line by well-meaning, Christ-following athletes that we have become ignorant as to what it actually means or looks like. We throw it around robotically—knowing we are supposed to say it but unaware of what it means.

As a result, we may be unintentionally offending the infinite God of the universe. It can be very foolish to use a word without understanding the full depth of its meaning, especially one as important as *glory*. Though unintentional, our ignorance surrounding the word *glory* can potentially lead us into three dangerous traps. By no means is this an attempt to pigeonhole every Christian athlete who has ever used the phrase "glory to God." These are dangers we can fall prey to, however, when we have a distorted view of glory.

Danger #1: Prideful Redirection

We've all seen it plenty of times. An athlete makes a fantastic play. The crowd goes crazy. The athlete celebrates with his or her teammates. After the game, the interview follows a predictable script:

Media: "Can you walk us through that play you just made?"

Athlete: "I mean, I want to start by giving all the glory to God and thank him for this moment."

This is called redirecting praise. Somebody offers you a compliment and you attempt to deflect praise by giving credit to someone else. What possible danger is there in that?

Acts 14 gives us some insight into this. Paul and Barnabas are in a city called Lystra, and Paul heals a guy who has been unable to walk since birth. Let's begin in verse 11:

> And when the crowds saw what Paul had done, they lifted up their voices, saying in Lycaonian, 'The gods have come down to us in the likeness of men!' Barnabas they called Zeus, and Paul, Hermes, because he was the chief speaker. And the priest of Zeus, whose temple was at the entrance to the city, brought oxen and garlands to the gates and wanted to offer sacrifice with the crowds" (Acts 14:11–13).

Athlete, can you recognize what is going on in this scenario? Let's recap. Paul and Barnabas do something amazing that draws the attention of the crowd. The crowd goes crazy, screaming their names and comparing them to the all-time greats. Maybe they even did the wave. This type of behavior happens every week in our sports-saturated culture.

Paul and Barnabas have a great response. They do not say, "All the glory to God!" They do not say, "Thanks, guys. We just want to take a second to thank our Lord and Savior Jesus Christ." They didn't double-fist pound their chests and then point to the sky. Instead, they run to the scene and plead with the crowd to stop worshiping them. Paul and Barnabas did not buy into their hype. Even though the crowd cheered them on, they actively pushed against the praise.

My fear is that our "all glory to God" refrain after the game has become nothing more than a Christian way of saying, "Thank you for the compliment."

Paul and Barnabas understood the danger of being praised and worshiped. Remember, Acts 14 occurs after Acts 12. In chapter 12, Herod was killed immediately after failing to give glory to God. Paul and Barnabas aggressively attacked the praise lavished on them and sought to get the spotlight off of themselves.

Danger #2: Heartless Dedication

Another danger we can fall into is that of heartless dedication. The concept here is pretty simple. We claim to play our sports to glorify God or as a grateful response for what he has done for us. Many Christian athletes will use the phrase AO1 (audience of one) as a way of saying they play for God.

If that's truly the case, great! My fear, however, is that we have become a subculture of Christianity that gives excellent lip service to our intentions, when in reality our hearts are not centered on God or even thinking about him at all. If you are claiming to compete for an audience of one but your words aren't backed up by your heart attitude and your actions throughout the competition and daily rhythms of your sport, I want to plead with you—please be careful.

Isaiah 1 paints a pretty terrifying picture of how God responds to this kind of hypocrisy. The people of God are offering sacrifices, throwing parties and festivals as prescribed by the law. They are doing and saying all the right things.

But there is a problem.

God is not a fan. In fact, he actually says he *hates* it at a soul level (Isa. 1:14).

The people of God had fallen into the dangerous trap of heartless dedication. They were saying the right things. They were even doing some of the right things. If it were today, they probably would be tweeting the right things, too. But the connection between their hearts and their hands was severed. Rehearsing the right phrases or words does not score any brownie points with a jealous God who wants more than our lip service.

Danger #3: End Product over Process

A third danger we can fall prey to when we don't fully understand what glory is and how to give it to God is that we can misunderstand what God really desires from us.

Have you ever noticed *when* we give glory to God?

Game-winning play? Yep.

Big performance? Yep.

Losing a big game? Nope.

In the midst of an injury? Nope.

We wrongly assume that God primarily gets the glory when we play well or win.

Does he want us to play with excellence? Absolutely. I would argue (and I do in chapter 6) that doing so reflects his image very well.

The problem, however, is that we often believe God is more glorified through the person who hit the game-winning shot than through the defender who gave it everything he had and failed. We have made a dangerous link between earthly success and the primary way God is glorified.

First Samuel 16 shows us the main thing God is after. God sends Samuel to choose the next king of Israel from among

Jesse's sons. Predictably, Jesse brings out the son he thinks is the best option. Here's how the scene plays out:

> When they came, he looked on Eliab and thought, "Surely the LORD's anointed is before him." But the Lord said to Samuel, "Do not look on his appearance or on the height of his stature, because I have rejected him. For the LORD sees not as man sees: man looks on the outward appearance, but the LORD looks on the heart" (1 Sam. 16:6–7).

In a SportsCenter top-plays culture, we are easily deceived into believing that what impresses us must also impress God. It's an easy mistake to make. But it's not one without consequences.

These three dangers are the result of our wrong assumptions about glory. As was the case with my friend badly misunderstanding what he was saying, we must have a clear understanding of what we're talking about if we want to give God what he desires most. It's literally a weighty concept (which we'll talk more about) and not to be taken lightly.

In a sports center top-plays culture, we are easily deceived into believing that what impresses us must also impress God. It's an easy mistake to make. But it's not one without consequences.

A Way Forward

The defensive end had just sacked the quarterback to effectively end the game and send his team to the NFC championship. The reporter found him at mid-field, and what follows is their interaction (as best I can remember it).

Reporter: "Congratulations on a great game. Can you take us through that last play?"

Athlete: "Thanks. I just want to give all glory to God...all glory to God!"

Reporter: "There was not much talk about you personally leading up to the game. It seems like maybe they forgot about you. How much did that motivate you out there today?"

Athlete: "All week long everybody was talking about how they were going to walk all over us. Nobody knew who I was. I kept telling myself all week that they will remember me after the game. Everyone will know my name!"

All glory to God! Everyone will know my name! This athlete may have said some of the right things, but he proved he didn't really know (or really mean) what he was saying when he went from glory to God to glory to himself in the blink of an eye.

He is not alone. Not too long ago I stood in front of seventy Christian athletes and asked them two simple questions. What does glory mean? How can we give it to God? My suspicion was proved correct. Nobody knew what they were talking about.

We need to learn what we are actually saying when using the word *glory* in the context of sports if we want to use it in a way that honors God. Both the church and Christian culture do a fairly good job letting athletes know that their sport is an opportunity to glorify God. What is lacking, however, is a detailed explanation of what that actually means. Trying to nail down a concrete definition of this common word is tricky.

For starters, we can't point to a passage in scripture where it is clearly defined like we can with the word *faith* in Hebrews 11:1.

Another reason is that some things are difficult to describe. For example, suppose I ask you to describe soccer to a friend. What would you say?[3] It might go something like this. You play the game with a round ball, filled with air. Usually the ball is checkered in black and white. The game occurs on a big field with a large goal on either end. The team with the ball passes it to each other using anything on their body except their hands. The object is to get the ball into the opposing team's goal.

If you play soccer or are passionate about the game, you know my brief description doesn't come close to capturing the beauty and intricacy of the game. Nevertheless, the listener would at least have a very basic understanding of the game without ever having seen it played. They could now imagine it (on some level, anyway) based on what you told them.

Now, what if I asked you to explain the word *happiness*? Or the color red? Or the number three? A little more difficult to do, isn't it? We often know what it is when we see it or experience it, but it would be very hard for us to clearly define any of those with clarity.

Similarly, describing *glory* at a basic level like we might describe soccer is not possible. It's more like trying to describe the color red to a person who is blind. So we need to consider it from a few different angles to get a better picture of what glory is, especially in the context of sports. To that end, we'll look at three increasingly complex concepts that ultimately build on each other: glory, God's glory, and giving God glory.

What Is Glory?

Glory simply means *weight*. It means a particular object is heavy. A house has more glory than a cardboard box. A car has more glory than a bicycle. A rock has more glory than a piece of paper. Take a cup of water and drop a small piece of paper in it. What happens? Probably not much. Maybe you will see a small ripple. Now what if you dropped a rock in the same cup of water? Big splash. Water on the table. Maybe the water gets on the floor or on you. Here's the point—Glory is a measurement of the weightiness or robustness of an object. The more glory an object has, the more it will affect the environment around it and cause people to notice.

Glory simply means weight.

What Is God's Glory?

As these concepts become increasingly complex, my ability to explain them decreases. To define God's glory, I'm going to lean heavily on the thoughts of these pastors and theologians: Tim Keller and John Piper. Let's start with Keller. He states that God's glory is "at least the combined magnitude of all God's attributes and qualities put together."[4] In a sense, what Keller is saying is that God's glory is the combined weight of everything that makes God *God*. His love, justice, goodness, wrath, omniscience, omnipotence, majesty, wisdom, and grace are all aspects of who he is, and when combined are "at least" what makes up his glory.

Piper unpacks God's glory this way:

> What is it? I believe the glory of God is the going public of his infinite worth. I define the holiness of God as the infinite value of God, the infinite intrinsic worth of God. And when that goes public in creation, the heavens are telling the glory of God, and human beings are manifesting his glory, because we're created in his image, and we're trusting his promises so that we make him look gloriously trustworthy."[5]

If we combine Keller's and Piper's definitions of God's glory, we could conclude that his glory is, at least, the weight of everything that makes him God *and* the going public of that weight for others to notice.

The big (glorious!) question that remains for athletes is this: In light of how much glory God already has, how can we possibly *give* glory to God through our sports?

What Does It Mean to Give God Glory?

Giving glory to God certainly doesn't mean that we can somehow add to his glory by what we do or say. God is not lacking in glory; in fact, God is not lacking in anything. That's a foundational truth that actually frees us from inflated views of our own importance.

To get this concept, it might be helpful to look at how this plays out in sports. Think of Lebron James. When fans chant his name, cheer him on, and, in an odd sense, worship him, they are not making him a better basketball player. He is already an incredible basketball player. When fans cheer for him and talk about his greatness as a basketball player, they are going public with the truth about him so others can know and be affected by it, too. See the difference? What he does on the court makes him a great basketball player. The fans give him glory by acknowledging his greatness.

So giving God glory means *thinking and acting in a way that pleases God and draws attention to who he is.* As an athlete, you bring glory to God when you think and act in a way that pleases God and draws attention to who he is.

As an athlete, you bring glory to God when you think and act in a way that pleases God and draws attention to who he is.

If we are supposed to give God glory, we need to make sure we have a proper perspective about ourselves and God. Only when we understand who the key players are in this process can we truly move forward to learn how to give God what he wants through our sports. So in the next chapter, we'll focus on who God is and why he is worthy of receiving glory.

CHAPTER 2

ON GOD

*What comes into our minds when we think about God
is the most important thing about us.*

—A. W. Tozer

How is an athlete supposed to view a God who desires glory more than anything else?

If we are to give God what he wants most, we first need to see him through the right lens. Why is this necessary? For us to know what he wants, we first need to know who he truly is. This can be difficult, of course. He is infinite and we are limited. Yet there is much that he has revealed about himself that we can understand. Without a biblical understanding of who God is, we can easily default to three unhealthy views of him. These false perspectives ultimately do more harm than good and inhibit our ability to glorify him.

The first of this unholy trinity of poor perspectives is to view God as being distant and uninvolved in some aspects of life. The lie we believe—or have been told—is that God does not care about sports. He cares about a lot of things, including us, but he is far too busy to be concerned with something as silly as a game. We may be able to give God glory, but it will probably have nothing to do with how we prepare for and play the game. We imagine that God is only concerned about the platform that sports gives us to share his love with other people. The danger of this view of God is that it can ruin your motivation for playing. After all, if he desires glory in all things yet doesn't care about your sport, you are wasting his time and yours.

We see in the Gospel accounts that God pursues us relentlessly, even sending his son to die for us. Moreover, the parables and stories, not to mention the rest of the New Testament, portray a God whose interest in us extends far beyond what we might call religious activities to include all of life.

Dr. Ed Uszynski, who has worked with elite athletes for the last three decades and currently serves as the Lead Strategist and Content Developer for the AthletesinAction.org website, wrote:

> A crucified yet victorious Christ should be proof enough that God doesn't operate with the same definitions of winning and losing as humans. But God most certainly does care who wins—just not at all in the same way we do and certainly not in the way implied by most post-game interviews. He cares about everything that happens in the universe. His sovereignty extends to the atomic level, where every atom of every cell arranges itself in relation to every other according to His plans and purposes.[1]

Perhaps Abraham Kuyper summed it up best when he said, "There is not a square inch in the whole domain of our human existence over which Christ, who is Sovereign over all, does not cry 'Mine!'"[2]

The point is that God is not indifferent about anything that takes place within his universe, which includes how you play and think about your sport. He cares!

The second perspective we can default to is to view God as a genie. Nobody would ever admit this, but our prayer life and actions leading up to a competition often reveal this perspective. The lie we believe is that God can be used or manipulated. We all have tried this before. In the days leading up to a big competition, you decide to be extra obedient. Maybe you pray more. Maybe you read your Bible more. Maybe you stop looking at certain images on the Internet or social media. The reason you do this is to get God in your good graces so he will bless you when the competition comes. You probably aren't even fully aware of your motivations. In any case, it's okay to admit it if you have done this. I've done it, too.

Tim Keller, in his book *The Prodigal God*, talks about why this lie is so dangerous. "If, like the elder brother, you seek to control God through your obedience, then all your morality is just a way to use God to make him give you the things in life you really want."[3] For God to be glorified, our primary focus needs to shift to what *he* wants. Our futile attempts to impress God into blessing us show that we misunderstand the essence of the gospel. The gospel shows us that God is pleased with us, not because of anything we do or have done but because of what Jesus has already done for us.

Completing the trifecta of poor perspectives on God is seeing him like you see your Instagram audience. There is a reason you take a picture. And then retake it. And then retake it. And then doctor it up and slap a filter on it until it is perfect. To get the maximum amount of attention...er...engagement, you figure you need to put your best stuff out there. You think what your audience truly wants is premium content of you.

When we choose to give glory to God, we are telling how we view him. For most athletes, we give God glory after we have done something great. A game-clinching play. A personal best. A championship. There's certainly nothing wrong with redirecting praise when it is wrongly directed at us. I believe the danger lies in thinking God cares about athletic success more than he actually does.

> *I believe the danger lies in thinking God cares about athletic success more than he actually does.*

The assumption can be that in God's economy, earthly awards and success are of the highest value to him, that he somehow needs our success in order for him to be the most glorified. By choosing to give God his due only after our success, we reinforce the idea that he is no different than a fan, a coach, or an owner. He's out to win. Period. We make a false connection between our victories and God's approval.

Again, the gospel shines a light on this lie. The beautiful and scandalous truth of Romans 5:8 is that "God shows his love for us in that while we were still sinners, Christ died for us." *While we were still sinners.* Not when we cleaned up our act. Not when we were on a winning streak. At our worst, not our best. At our low point, at our point of failure, God steps in and saves us. By *that* he is glorified.

If we are going to move forward in using sports as a vehicle to drive us closer to God, we need to have an accurate understanding of who he is and what he cares about most. Only then will we begin to understand what really pleases him.

How Does God Want Us to View Him?

Paul never penned a letter to the church at Lambeau Field or in Madison Square Garden, so we will never fully know how God views athletic achievements, especially those "given" to him. We do get a glimpse of how God desires to be seen through the life of Jesus and his many parables. God identifies himself not as a fan but as our Father.

In J. I. Packer's classic book, *Knowing God,* he answers the question: What is a Christian? "The question can be answered in many ways, but the richest answer I know is that a Christian is one who has God as Father."[4]

This is not only good news for us as Christians, but also for us as Christians who happen to be athletes. God has revealed himself as Father, which is a relational description we're familiar with, even if we've only known imperfect fathers. So we can take the question, "How does God view athletes when they try to give him glory?" and translate it to "How does an excellent father see his children when they do good things in his honor?"

A View of God from My Refrigerator

I have a six-year-old son who loves to color. Sunday school is where he releases his weekly masterpieces that end up on our refrigerator. I think there are some significant parallels in how I experience my son's art and how God experiences and receives our athletic endeavors.

Perspective

I know my son has a high opinion of his artwork. He worked hard on it, and in his eyes, it truly is a masterpiece. Here's the thing: he's only six. He has no idea what constitutes impressive artwork. With that said, for someone his age to color within the lines is admirable. But it's no Monet. It's no Rembrandt. Nobody comes into my house and notices his artwork in the kitchen. Nobody snaps a picture of it and puts it on Instagram with the hashtag #ForDadsGlory or #ForDadsHouse. While my son thinks he is adding value to my home with each stroke of his crayon, all it really is in my eyes is...cute. It's endearing.

Athlete, as you strive to become the best and bring glory to God through your athletic accomplishments, it would be wise for you to keep your results in perspective. If a person is a good steward of the gifts God has given to him or her, that's admirable. But first and foremost, let's remember the greatness of the Giver of those gifts. Let's remember to focus on him more than on what we're doing for him. He is the one who created the universe. He parted the Red Sea. He knows the names of every star. Nothing happens in his creation without his approval. Our heavenly Father knows all things past, present, and future, including the hearts and the minds of every person who has ever lived. Against this backdrop, our athletic performances are...endearing. Saying that is not to diminish our ability to give glory to God but to increase our view of God.

Process

Why do I love my son's drawings? Simple. He draws for *me*. I am at the forefront of his mind when he carefully adds color to the paper.

"Daddy will love this."

"Daddy really likes it when I use this color."

"Daddy picks me up and spins me around every time I make him something. I am going to make this one the best yet."

What I love about my son's artwork is not the result, but the process of him doing it. I love his attention to detail. I love that he is not comparing his drawing to the work of other six-year-olds. I love it that he makes me wait ten minutes later than any other parent picking up their kid because he wants so badly to make sure everything is just right. We can get so wrapped up in the results of our athletic competitions that we can forget what actually brings glory to God—our heart attitudes throughout the competition and the way we conduct ourselves.

Perfection

This point is cliché, but it needs to be said. I don't love my son's drawings because they are the best ones in the class. Nothing would change the way I feel about them. Regardless of what the teacher says about them or how they compare to the rest of the class, my feelings about his creative attempts would not change.

I love his drawings because I love him. I love them because I know that he made them for me. Regardless of whether they stink or are perfect, my heart attitude toward my son remains the same. I have a daughter who likes to color too. As a father, how would I feel if everyone in the class applauded my son's impressive art (for a six-year-old) and neglected my daughter's artwork because she cannot color within the lines? Would I not respond the same toward her as I do toward my son, regardless of what the results of her work looked like?

I'm concerned that we believe God is more glorified through the person who hit the game-winning three-pointer than the defender who gave it everything he had and failed to prevent the shot from going in. We have to break the link between earthly success and God receiving glory. This flawed thinking stems from a wrong perspective of who God is and what he values most. Fans cheer based on performance. Coaches evaluate based on what value you bring to the team. A good father's opinion of you relies on who he says you are as his son or daughter, not on what you do for him.

I'm concerned that we believe God is more glorified through the person who hit the game-winning three-pointer than the defender who gave it everything he had and failed to prevent the shot from going in.

Confession time. Before my son was born I never cared about art. I found it terribly boring. I had no desire to go to

Europe and see big fancy buildings and old paintings hanging in them. My opinion has changed since then. Why? Because art has become a vehicle through which my son expresses his love for me. I care a great deal about it now. Art has become a relational bond that my son and I share. I believe one of the primary reasons God cares about our sports is that they can be leveraged as a vehicle through which we can express our love to him (thus glorifying him).

Can you begin to see that how we view God matters? When we view God through the proper lens—as a father—it changes everything. Here's another choice passage from Packer's *Knowing God*:

> You sum up the whole of New Testament teaching in a single phrase, if you speak of it as a revelation of the Fatherhood of the holy Creator. In the same way, you sum up the whole of New Testament religion if you describe it as the knowledge of God as one's holy Father. If you want to judge how well a person understands Christianity, find out how much he makes of the thought of being God's child, and having God as his Father. If this is not the thought that prompts and controls his worship and prayers and his whole outlook on life, it means that he does not understand Christianity very well at all. For everything that Christ taught, everything that makes the New Testament new, and better than the Old, everything that is distinctively Christian as opposed to merely Jewish, is summed up in the knowledge of the Fatherhood of God. "Father" is the Christian name for God.[5]

For many of you reading this, your lack of a good father figure or disdain for your earthly dad makes this perspective shift difficult to embrace. Regardless of whether you have an amazing earthly dad or something less than that, God is a perfect Father, infinitely better than the best earthly father.

For those of us who struggle to see God as Father, how can we grow in this area? Questions like that are among those this book hopes to answer. I want to continue to delve into biblical perspectives on sports and life and also provide some practical tips to move us from the old ways of seeing and acting to the new, better ways God has for us. To that end, here are some practical suggestions for growing in your experience of seeing God as your heavenly Father.

Memorize Scripture

Pastor and author Charles Swindoll is a big fan of this practice. He wrote in his book *Growing Strong in the Seasons of Life*:

> I know of no other single practice in the Christian life more rewarding, practically speaking, than memorizing Scripture....No other single exercise pays greater spiritual dividends! Your *prayer life* will be strengthened. Your *witnessing* will be sharper and much more effective....Your *attitudes* and *outlook* will begin to change. Your *mind* will become alert and observant. Your *confidence* and *assurance* will be enhanced. Your *faith* will be solidified.[6]

Memorizing scripture verses that remind you of God's identity as a Father can be one of the most effective ways to transform how you view God. There are plenty of verses that depict God as our Father that are worth memorizing, but two good ones to start with are 2 Corinthians 1:3 and 1 John 3:1.

Call God "Daddy"

Romans 8:15–16 says, "For you did not receive the spirit of slavery to fall back into fear, but you have received the Spirit of adoption as sons, by whom we cry, 'Abba! Father!' The Spirit himself bears witness with our spirit that we are children of God." The word *Abba* is equivalent to *Daddy*. One easy way to begin recognizing God as Father is to address him as Daddy when you pray. It may sound awkward at first, but give it a try. In addition to transforming your view of God, calling him Daddy (at least some of the time) will also help shape the content of your prayers.

Pause before You Pray or Read

Pausing before you pray or read is another really easy way to shape your view of God as your Father. Before you read the Bible or enter into a time of prayer, stop for 15 seconds and just sit in silence. As you sit, envision God as your Father. Ask yourself what it feels like to have a perfect Father caring for you at all times.

Write Father on Your Cleats, Hand, or Wrist

Writing the word *Father* or even *F* someplace that you will regularly see it will help you focus on who you are giving glory to through your sport. We will dig into this concept further in chapter 4, but this will serve as a visual reminder for you. Deuteronomy 11:18 is a good example of this practice.

What Is the Gospel?

Before we go any further, we really need to make sure we understand the basic gospel message. It's a message that starts with some bad news before getting to the best news the world has ever heard.

First Things First

The bad news—We do not enter this world as children of God. None of us do. The Bible actually says we "were by nature children of wrath" (Ephesians 2:3).

It gets worse. The gap that separates us from God is caused by our sin. We are all guilty of it according to Romans 3:23.

And it gets even worse. Romans 6:23 says there is a penalty to pay for our disobedience. "For the wages of sin is death."

To sum it up, we are born, not as God's children, but as objects of his wrath because of our sin. And the price we must pay for that sin is death. That's the bad news. So who's ready for some good news?

Gospel actually means *good news*, so we'll refer to it as such. Romans 6:23 does not end with doom and gloom. There is always a *but* with God. In its entirety, the verse reads: "For the wages of sin is death, but the free gift of God is eternal life in Christ Jesus our Lord." We sin and deserve death. God sends his son, Jesus, to the earth. He lives a life without sin and dies the death we deserve. Then God raises him from the dead! Jesus's death satisfies the price that we owed for our sin.

And, it's *completely free*. That's the definition of grace—free gift!

You become a child of God—a Christian—when you respond to this gift by confessing with your mouth that Jesus is Lord and believing in your heart that God raised him from the dead (Romans 10:9). When you become a child of God, you have the blessing and privilege of calling God your Father.

As we continue to consider how sports can drive us closer to God, we need to leave our performance-based mindset in the rearview mirror. By no means does that mean we should not strive to be the best we can be in our sports. It just means that excellence is not the only thing God is concerned with—or the only way we can give him glory. How, then, can we glorify God through sports? Before we look at practical ways we can do this, we must make one last realignment. And it deals with how we think about ourselves.

CHAPTER 3

ON ATHLETES

*I'm speaking to you out of deep gratitude for all
that God has given me, and especially as I have
responsibilities in relation to you. Living then, as
every one of you does, in pure grace, it's important
that you not misinterpret yourselves as people who are
bringing this goodness to God. No, God brings it all
to you. The only accurate way to understand ourselves
is by what God is and by what he does for us, not by
what we are and what we do for him.*

—Romans 12:3 (The Message)

Lions. Dragons. Eagles. Wolves. I have even seen tattoos of beasts resembling something straight out of Revelation. Athletes get some crazy tattoos. Most tattoos tell us something about the individual. Whether it's something about their past, present, or aspirations for the future, tattoos give us a small glimpse into how people want to be defined. Aside from those done after a long night of impaired thinking, tattoos are never random. There is a deep intentionality to them. If you are ever looking for a conversation starter, just ask someone what their tattoo means.

Tattoos say something about our identity—and when it comes to our identity, there will always be competing voices in our head. Whether you invite those voices in or not, you as an athlete will always have parents, coaches, fans, social media avatars, and sometimes your own conscience telling you who you are. And the voices we hear are never neutral. They either build us up or tear us down. You have probably experienced both in your life.

The fortunate among us have had those negative voices countered by positive Christian messages such as:

You are strong in Christ!

God has your back!

God loves you no matter what!

Phrases like these can be helpful. They encourage you to feel better about yourself based on truths gleaned from the Bible. That's both good and right. But I want to press in a little further by deconstructing a cultural norm and reconstructing it into something that I believe is far more helpful. Just because those phrases are good doesn't mean they're the best.

Our culture, both secular and Christian, is obsessed with self-esteem. We have reduced the definition of self-esteem to anything that falls under the banner of feeling good about yourself. For example, consider how youth sports have changed. No more keeping score. No winners. No losers. Everyone gets a trophy. Don't forget your orange slices and juice boxes on the way out. Why? Because heaven forbid if we send a kid home feeling sad because he or she lost or got schooled by someone who was better.

We have become addicted to the drug of affirmation and high self-esteem. Neither of them is bad, but as with any drug, they can mess with our minds and move us to places where we become reliant on them at all costs.

Why is this a bad thing? Because pride and despair grow in the toxic soil of the self-esteem movement. It's a movement that ultimately encourages us to find our worth in the opinions of others since how we view ourselves is so heavily influenced by what others think of us. Athletes typically grow up in an environment characterized by parents, coaches, fans, friends, and teammates constantly giving praise or rebuke based on their performance. Again, the voices we hear are never neutral.

Athletes, with the "help" of these voices, tend to gravitate toward either pride or despair. Pride is usually pretty easy to spot. A prideful person is typically boastful and self-promoting. We have all seen athletes who are full of themselves. One of the worst things about pride is how difficult it is to see it in ourselves.

The other expression of performance-based-self-esteem-run-amok is sneakier and not so quickly identifiable. It is wounded pride taking the form of self-pity and pouting. While not as brazen as boastful pride, it is nevertheless just as self-absorbed.

In his book *Desiring God*, John Piper describes these two forms of pride:

> Boasting is the response of pride to success. Self-pity is the response of pride to suffering. Boasting says, "I deserve admiration because I have achieved so much." Self-pity says, "I deserve admiration because I have sacrificed so much." Boasting is the voice of pride in the heart of the strong. Self-pity is the voice of pride in the heart of the weak. Boasting sounds self-sufficient. Self-pity sounds self-sacrificing. The reason self-pity does not look like pride is that it appears to be needy. But the need arises from a wounded ego....The need self-pity feels does not come

from a sense of unworthiness, but from a sense of unrecognized worthiness. It is the response of unapplauded pride.[1]

The boastful athlete relishes the approval and affirmation of others and lives off the temporal high that it produces.

The self-pitying athlete is desperate for the same drug. He or she is going through praise withdrawal. A shot of self-esteem is the quick fix that so many run after.

You are strong in Christ!

God has your back!

God loves you no matter what!

Again, those statements are right and true. But I fear they are too often used as a quick fix to low self-esteem rather than as a gospel aid to recalibrating our identity in Christ.

You know what tattoo I haven't seen on an athlete yet? A tattoo of a sheep.[2] Yet that is precisely how the people of God are pictured in the Bible—not as lions or other ferocious predators, but as sheep.

> *You know what tattoo I haven't seen on an athlete yet? A tattoo of a sheep.[2] Yet that is precisely how the people of God are pictured in the Bible—not as lions or other ferocious predators, but as sheep.*

A quick Google search can tell you a lot about the unique characteristics of sheep. Here are some of the highlights I found, if you want to call them highlights. Sheep are dumb. They are prey for just about everything. They are slow. They are constantly fearful. They blindly follow the sheep in front of them. They are foolish, slow to learn, and stubborn.

Tim Challies, a popular Christian blogger, had this to say about sheep: "Do a little bit of reading about sheep and you'll soon see they are not survivors. They are not strong and independent creatures, not proud hunters or fierce predators.

They're actually kind of pathetic, entirely dependent upon a shepherd for at least three reasons."[3]

He suggests that the three defining characteristics of sheep are that they are dumb, directionless, and defenseless. Not much to be proud of in that list.

Regarding a sheep's level of intelligence, Max Lucado points out, "When a swarm of nose flies appears, sheep panic. They run. They hide. They toss their heads up and down for hours. They forget to eat. They aren't able to sleep. Ewes stop milking, and lambs stop growing. The entire flock can be disrupted, even destroyed by the presence of a few flies."[4] Yes, sheep are dumb.

Sheep also tend to get lost a lot. For no apparent reason, they just walk away from the herd, from their shepherd. They usually get into trouble out there by themselves and often don't make it on their own. Challies said, "Put a sheep in the wild and you've just given nature a snack."[5]

Nothing is empowering or encouraging about being called a sheep. It might even be a little offensive to some. A sheep represents everything that an athlete should not be.

And yet the Bible often refers to us as sheep. God doesn't position us to give him glory by raising our self-esteem but by revealing our real need for him in every aspect of our lives. In a culture that consistently tells Christian athletes to leverage their platform for the glory of God, we would do well to remember that throughout scripture, God often used weak, insignificant, lowly people to do his will. Sheep-like people, not self-sufficient superstars, seem to be among God's favorites. In fact, there are many instances in the Bible when the people of God would come to him with expressions of their inadequacy, and not once did he tell them how awesome they were.

Consider Moses. God's people were slaves at the hands of the Egyptians for 400 years. God appointed Moses as his instrument to free the people and lead them to the Promised Land. What an incredible opportunity. Moses was going to be The Guy. But he was afraid. As God reveals himself to Moses in a burning bush, Moses has second thoughts. He begins to doubt himself. As someone who regularly disciples and mentors college athletes, I often have a response that's different than God's. I encourage men who struggle with self-confidence. I try to lift their spirits in seasons of doubt and frustration. God takes a different approach with Moses. Five times Moses says "but" and offers an excuse for not being able to accomplish the task. Not once does God address the insecurities of Moses, but rather God turns Moses's attention to what God can do through him. God didn't respond to Moses's fears by saying, "You can do this!" His response was always, "Hey, dummy, just trust me" (my paraphrase).

I love that. God affirms that Moses *was* right. He *couldn't* do it. He was not quick on his feet. He was not in need of a pump-up talk. His self-esteem didn't need a boost. What he was feeling was true. He was a mere sheep, inadequate and insignificant on his own and in need of a shepherd.

Our culture tries to feed you the medicine of self-esteem and affirmation when you feel unworthy. Feeling unworthy and inadequate to handle the challenges of living in a broken world on your own is not a disease. It is the mark of a healthy state of mind and soul. Prideful sheep do not last long on their own. We were created to be led by a shepherd. Recognizing that is not weakness—it's humility. And it is an essential heart attitude we need to address if we have any hope of bringing glory to God through our sports.

Athlete, having confidence is one thing. Walking with a swagger is another. This type of pride is an affront to the gospel. Know this: Testing God's patience by continuing to walk in such a way is a very unwise path. Something needs to change. The antidote for the poison of pride is a humble heart. In light of

God's greatness and our complete dependence on him for life and breath and everything we've been given, humility is the only sane posture in which to live.

Aside from the Bible encouraging us to be humble, studies show that people who practice humility are happier, healthier, and more optimistic about life. This should not surprise us. When we live in accordance with reality, things are bound to go better for us.

Despite the encouragement that God gives us to be humble and the sociological evidence to its benefits, it can be hard to practice humility in the midst of the daily grind of our sports. Our ability to be humble often ebbs and flows with the circumstances in front of us.

Humility is like a muscle—it gets stronger if we consistently give it attention and push it beyond its current level of comfort. Conversely, if we fail to exercise it habitually, our ability to be humble atrophies.

> *Humility is like a muscle—it gets stronger if we consistently give it attention and push it beyond its current level of comfort.*

Here are seven habits of humble athletes, mental choices you can incorporate into your daily life to grow and maintain your humility "muscles."

Humble Athletes Take Time to Soak in the Moment

Before a practice or competition, humble athletes stop, take a deep breath, and make it a point to appreciate what they are about to engage in. Who else on this earth gets to play a game they love in front of fans who cheer them on in the process?

Is there pressure involved in that? Sure. But humble athletes make it a habit to pause and enjoy, if only for a moment, the unique opportunity they get to experience.

Humble Athletes Recognize People Who Go Unnoticed

Humble athletes shake the hand of the maintenance worker who helps cut the grassy field they are about to tear up with their cleats or the janitor who mops the floor so their feet won't slide on the dust. They write their athletic trainer a thank you note for taping them up, helping them rehab, or stretching them out before practice. They give a hug to the diehard fan who is at every game and cheers for their team regardless of the outcome. Humble athletes understand that the world does not revolve around them, and they make sure their actions reflect that.

Humble Athletes Fight against Entitlement

Humble athletes recognize every blessing they receive as a gift rather than something they deserve or have earned. Entitlement is the cousin of pride and stands in direct opposition to humility.

Per diem money on a road trip. New shoes. New gear. Laundry washed and dried. Water or Gatorade from a trainer. Tutors helping them pass their classes. Teachers giving them grace because of their travel schedule.

Humble athletes fight against the "I deserve" mentality that is so pervasive in our culture by thanking the givers of these gifts and frequently checking the posture of their hearts.

Humble Athletes Are Coachable

Humble athletes listen to advice and instruction from their coaches and, when appropriate, from their fellow teammates. They realize they do not have all the answers. Even if they disagree with the input, it does not keep them from at least testing it out on the field. The prideful heart says through boasting, "I know it all," or through self-pity, "I know nothing." The humble heart says, "I want to learn more. Help!" Humble athletes have an appreciation for the authority they're under (coaches) and a desire to soak up any knowledge they can.

Humble Athletes Are Honest with Reality

Humble athletes understand that life is not always going to be rainbows and butterflies. There will be hardships in the form of injuries, losses, poor performances, and team conflicts.

Pride causes us to wear a mask and implore a fake-it-until-you-make-it mentality. Humility stares reality in the face and recognizes it for what it is. Humble athletes do not pretend these circumstances do not exist or pretend they are not affected by them. They do, however, in the midst of the struggle, constantly ask themselves, "What good can come from this or has already come from this?"

In both the high and low times in sports, humility can be tough to maintain. Humble athletes make an effort to step back, look at the bigger picture, and find perspective in light of their relationship with God and what's most important in life.

Humble Athletes' Joy Is Not Conditional

Humble athletes don't need a win or an epic personal best to practice humility. Humility for the humble athlete is not dependent on good results, nor is it circumstantial. They understand that lasting joy is unattainable in a game that delivers both the highest of highs and the lowest of lows.

So how do they set themselves on a trajectory of consistent humility? They put their hope in the one who does not change—God. They read—no, devour his word. They participate—no, are actively involved in a community of like-minded people to sharpen one another. They pray. They confess. Most of all, they stay connected to the one who calls himself the Good Shepherd.

Humble Athletes Recognize Excellence in Their Opponent

Have you ever noticed that rivals tend to bring their best to the table when they play? Humble athletes practice humility toward a rival on two levels. One, they are thankful their opponent will ultimately bring out the best in their own performance. And two, because their joy is not dependent on winning, they can appreciate and look forward to the competition itself. Humble athletes have a unique ability to want to beat their opponent while at the same time appreciating the intensity of the competition.

Sheep who truly know they are sheep understand they are nothing without a shepherd. He is what makes them safe, significant, and worthy. But the order in which they understand that is crucial. If they start by saying they are safe, significant, and worthy, they may soon forget they are sheep and wander off. Sheep must first understand their identity as sheep. Then and only then can they talk about the glorious privileges that come with being connected to the shepherd. And those privileges are glorious.

Kevin Black, wrestling coach, founder, and owner of the Victory School of Wrestling, had some great reminders of what is true about you because of your relationship with the Good Shepherd. Remember, these truths are not meant to be a self-esteem boost, but a realignment of your true identity.

> I am Loved (1 Thessalonians 1:4)
> I am Accepted (Romans 15:7)
> I am Complete (2 Corinthians 12:9)
> I am Bold & Confident (Ephesians 3:12)
> I am Made Alive (Ephesians 2:4–5)
> I am Valuable (1 Corinthians 7:23, Luke 12:24)
> I am a New Creation (2 Corinthians 5:17)
> I am a Masterpiece (Ephesians 2:10)
> I am Justified (Romans 3:24)
> I am Redeemed (Ephesians 1:7)
> I am Wise (1 Corinthians 1:30)
> I am Chosen (Ephesians 1:4)
> I am Precious (Isaiah 43:4)
> I am Fearfully & Wonderfully Made (Psalm 139:14)
> I am Set Free (Galatians 5:1)[6]

If these truths are used only to give us a boost of self-esteem, they will inevitably fail. They are meant to help us feel safe and free in the Shepherd's care. We have everything we could ever need through our relationship with Jesus. When we feel safe and free because of this relationship, we have the mindset we need to compete with authentic joy and passion. The author of a biography of Air Force fighter pilot John Boyd wrote, "Boyd said if a man can reduce his needs to zero, he is truly free: there is nothing that can be taken from him and nothing anyone can do to hurt him."[7]

Our grounding in who we are as sheep under the care of a Shepherd should assure us that our worth and purpose come from him, ultimately producing a peace that transcends all understanding (Phil. 4:7).

Athlete, God is our Father. God is our Shepherd. We are his sheep. That's the starting line. So what are some specific ways we can bring glory to God through sports? It's time to find out.

CHAPTER 4

ON MOTIVATION

Christ in me, I am enough.

—Helen Maroulis

I believe I know why you play your sport.

My confidence is based on the belief that beneath our lesser motivations, every athlete plays their particular sport for the same underlying reason. And if you are like thousands of other Christian athletes, at one point you have probably claimed Philippians 4:13 as a way to gain what you desire most. But Philippians 4:13 actually promises to deliver far more than we realize. We often claim it with the hope that God will enable us to experience some form of victory through maximum performance. God, however, offers us something much deeper and more satisfying than a short-lived success.

Before we look at the verse used by Christian athletes everywhere, ask yourself this question: What do you *really* want from your sports experience? When you perform well, what about that experience makes you want to come back for more? When you struggle or fail, what motivates you to either push forward or sink back? Why do you actually play your sport?

Maybe some of the following sentences resonate with your motivations:

> I play because I like winning.
> I play to feel the joy of playing.
> I play to gain my parents' approval.
> I play to experience my coach's approval.
> I play to garner fans' admiration.
> I play to impress the opposite sex.
> I play to make it to the next level.
> I play to impress my friends.

Did any of those strike a chord with you? Have you ever given serious thought to what drives you to play?

Growing up, I played sports to impress others. I loved it when I did well, and other people told me how great I was. As a runner, I literally chased after the admiration I sought from my parents, friends, and coaches. At the time, I would have identified impressing others as my primary motivation. I was wrong—there is a deeper motivation that drives us all. Only when we identify

Only when we identify what that deep-seated motivation is can we truly experience joy through our sports and give God the glory he is due.

what that deep-seated motivation is can we truly experience joy through our sports and give God the glory he is due.

Where does Philippians 4:13 fit into all of this? You may have this verse tattooed somewhere on your body. If you don't, you probably know someone who does.

> I can do all things through him who strengthens
> me.

What a great verse! I cannot even count how many times I prayed this verse as I toed the line for a track race. I have claimed this verse as if to say, "God, I know I can win this race because you will give me strength. It says so right in the Bible."

Let me introduce you to another passage of scripture.

> I rejoiced in the Lord greatly that now at length you have revived your concern for me. You were indeed concerned for me, but you had no opportunity. Not that I am speaking of being in need, for I have learned in whatever situation I am to be content. I know how to be brought low, and I know how to abound. In any and every circumstance, I have learned the secret of facing plenty and hunger, abundance and need" (Phil. 4:10–12).

If I were to ask you to sum up these three verses in a single word, what would that word be? How would you describe what the apostle Paul is trying to say to his readers?

Maybe the word you choose would be *contentment*.

Paul is saying that he has learned to be content in every situation. Whether he has a lot of success or a little, whether he is full or hungry, whether he is on top of the world or in the lowest of valleys, he has learned the secret of being content.

How is he able to do this? He provides the answer in the next verse: "I can do all things through him who strengthens me" (Phil. 4:13).

Is Paul talking about making the winning shot, winning a championship, or setting a new personal best? No. What he's saying, athlete, is that regardless of whether you succeed or fail in your sport—or at anything in life—you can find contentment in Christ. We wrongly claim Philippians 4:13 to help us succeed in sports, but what God is saying in this verse is that we already have everything we could ever need in Christ. More satisfying than gaining people's approval is getting to a place where you no longer need it. That's the real promise of this verse.

Our Ultimate Motivation

Are you ready to learn why you really play your sport? I would suggest that it's because you are seeking the elusive experience of contentment. That's at the bottom of all your hard work and striving for success. That's the dangling carrot in front of the lesser motivations you may have been able to identify.

The lie we believe is that Philippians 4:13 means that I can achieve any outcome in my sport because of Christ. We need to combat that lie with the truth that Philippians 4:13 means that I can have contentment regardless of the outcome because of Christ. There's a huge difference between the two.

> *The lie we believe is that Philippians 4:13 means that I can achieve any outcome in my sport because of Christ. We need to combat that lie with the truth that Philippians 4:13 means that I can have contentment regardless of the outcome because of Christ.*

The desire for contentment isn't a bad thing. It's a natural human desire. Who doesn't want to be content? The problem comes when we attempt to find contentment through sports achievements. That's a dead-end pursuit that will always leave us wanting more. If we are going to experience any lasting satisfaction through sports, the goal needs to be God himself, not particular outcomes. A game will never deliver true contentment. This doesn't mean that sports are bad or a waste of time. It only means that they were never intended to satisfy our hearts at the deepest level.

We will always end up disappointed when we try to use created things to find ultimate satisfaction. C. S. Lewis summarized this misdirected pursuit when he said this:

> It would seem that Our Lord finds our desires, not too strong, but too weak. We are half-hearted creatures, fooling about with drink and sex and ambition when infinite joy is offered us, like an ignorant child who wants to go on making mud pies in a slum because he cannot imagine what is meant by the offer of a holiday at the sea. We are far too easily pleased.[1]

Lewis suggests that instead of giving up on the idea of finding contentment, we should understand that too often we're simply expecting to get it from the wrong things. The beauty of Philippians 4:13 is that it offers us the proper route to reach the destination of contentment. It's right to claim the verse, but only in context, which is to say, only in the pursuit of a deeper joy that transcends our immediate circumstances.

As I said earlier, God has placed eternity in the hearts of man (Eccles. 3:11). That eternal void cannot be satisfied by the temporal things of this world. We need an eternal solution to satisfy our hearts. The contentment we long for is not found in a sport, a job, or an experience. It is found in a person. And his name is Jesus.

By this time in the book, this concept should not come as a surprise. If God desires glory, our motivation should be to give it to him. We can—and should—use sports as a vehicle to give him glory. Only then will we find a lasting joy that transcends circumstances.

Think of motivation as the steering wheel of your vehicle. When properly aligned, your car will naturally go straight. Conversely, when it is out of alignment, even a little bit, you will inevitably drift off course without even moving the wheel. In life, it does not take much for us to take our focus off of God. It's even easier for athletes in the midst of competition to forget why they're doing what they're doing. For most of us, the last thing we are thinking is how to be properly motivated in the heat of the moment. We want to win. We want to compete hard and with excellence. We are focused on the game itself, not on God. But the question of why we compete is often more important than the outcome itself.

Kurt Earl, founder of Compete4Christ, put it this way: "As Christians, we should care about being the best we can be, but we should care even more about making sure we don't lose sight of our 'why.' Why we compete is more important than how we compete."[2]

What Does This Look Like Practically?

On August 18, 2016, Helen Maroulis defeated Saori Yoshida from Japan, becoming the first female wrestler from the United States to win an Olympic gold medal. Yoshida was a 16-time consecutive world and Olympic gold medalist. She was unbeatable. Until she faced Maroulis.

In the months leading up to the Olympic Games, Maroulis was in a funk. Struggling with anxiety, fear, and a poor self-image, she knew something needed to happen internally to combat the negativity that consumed her thoughts. She began preaching to herself. She used the mantra "Christ is in me, and I am enough" as a rallying cry to drown out the voices in her head. She recited it out loud over and over again. She recited it while she practiced. She recited it while competing, clinging to the things that God said are true about her instead of the opinions of others. One of Maroulis's coaches described the internal motivational shift this way: "Helen had given herself permission to lay it all on the line on the biggest stage sports has to offer because her identity was secure. She was enough with or without that medal."[3]

Amazing! With our identity and motivation firmly grounded in Christ, we are not shaken by the outcome of a competition.

Free athletes will always compete at a higher level than those bogged down by the incessant need for others' approval.

We become freed up to compete without the fear of failure. Free athletes will always compete at a higher level than those bogged down by the incessant need for others' approval. It's important to note that coming to the point of inner contentment does not mean we let up in competition. Quite the opposite. Satisfaction in who Christ says we are gives us the green light to keep pushing forward. An inward contentment allows us to have an outward discontentment because it frees us from the chains of others' approval that hold us down.

When our motivation is properly aligned, our sports can lead us into further contentment in Christ. But if we get distracted, we fall prey to the trap of idolatry, expecting our sports to deliver things they can't, like long-term satisfaction. How is it possible for a competitive athlete trained to focus intently on his or her sport to drown out the outside noise? We need to retrain our minds to focus on God in a way that we consistently make sure our motivation is properly aligned, for God's glory and our own joy. This will not come naturally.

It takes a trigger.

The trigger is commonly referred to as a focal point. A focal point can be anything—a wristband, a tattoo, a watch. Writing on your shoes is another option. It could even be a scoreboard or a banner hung somewhere in the stadium. Ideally, this focal point will be something you consistently see in practice and during competitions.

In his book *The Handbook on Athletic Perfection*, Wes Neal helps explain how focal points can be a useful tool for Christian athletes. Neal describes a focal point as something you can quickly concentrate on that realigns your focus on your ultimate motivation to glorify God.[4] When I competed, I would write a Bible verse on my running shoes. Before every practice and competition, as I laced up my shoes, I would see the verse, and it would realign my thoughts to God. It was my daily reminder to bring my Father into these moments when I am naturally inclined to leave him out.

In addition to the challenge of actually remembering God when we participate in our sport is the challenge of finding the appropriate time to do so. For a wrestler, the time to realign your motivation is not when you are circling your opponent. For a football player, what happens mentally before the snap has a direct correlation to the play itself. So it's probably not the right time to realign your thoughts to God when you should be analyzing the opponent's formation. A golfer should give 100 percent of his or her focus to determine the break and speed of a particular putt. Depending on your sport, the best time to leverage the effectiveness of a focal point is when there is a pause in the action. In between quarters or periods is a good time. During halftime, in the middle of a timeout, or after a change of possession are other possibilities, depending on the sport. This will probably be uncomfortable at first. But, like anything, the more practice and attention you give to it, the more comfortable you will become using your focal point to realign your motivation.

This can be a new and challenging concept for some athletes to apply. Perhaps you have only trained your mind to zero in on the competition itself, blocking out everything else. As Christians, however, we are called to a higher standard than that. Focal points give us a practical way to move closer to that standard.

CHAPTER 5

ON WINNING

*The Christian shoemaker does his duty not by putting
little crosses on the shoes, but by making good shoes,
because God is interested in good craftsmanship.*

—Martin Luther

We need a better theology surrounding the topic of winning. There are too many questions and not enough answers. Is it okay for me to want to win? How does a Christian athlete approach the topic of winning? How much should an athlete care about it? At what point does an athlete cross over to the idol-infested waters of caring too much? Does God care if we pray for a win or for success? Can God be glorified through winning? If so, how?

This chapter will not answer all those questions, but it will hopefully move the ball forward in our understanding of how we should think about winning in light of the scriptures. We'll start by addressing some common errors.

Error #1 (from Christian Culture): Being Humble in Victory Means Not Celebrating

I was a D1 track/cross country runner, but I also have played golf recreationally since I was 15. To this day, I have not gotten any better, yet there is something about playing a game that is impossible to beat that continues to lure me back. On one particular fall day in Michigan, I learned that while you cannot beat the game, you can conquer individual holes.

I skulled it. At least that's what one of my friends told me as I watched my ball skip through the grass on the way to the green. It was a 143-yard par three. I had a new set of Nike knockoffs and went with an eight iron. The green sat above the tee box, so you couldn't tell if your shot made it up and settled nicely on the green or if it rolled off the back. Sand traps were situated on both sides of the green, inviting disaster.

There are few better feelings in the world of sport than hitting a golf ball clean and crisp, exactly as you envision it before lining up your shot. This was not one of those moments. As my club moved through its downward trajectory, I felt it before I saw it. The cold weather, combined with the reverberating steel shaft of the club, did no favors to my wimpy hands.

"Skulled it, huh?" my buddy remarked as the rest of the peanut gallery that made up my friends laughed. A skulled shot is when the front edge of the club face strikes the middle of the golf ball. The result is a ball that comes off the club fast and flat, with little to no spin and even less distance control. It's a horrible looking shot.

"Yep, that sucks," I replied, all the while trying to play it cool and not give them the satisfaction of knowing I hurt my hands in the process.

After resisting the urge to hit a second shot (nobody likes to hit a bad shot, especially on a par 3), I hopped into the golf cart and made my way up the hill to the green to survey the damage. I have a bad habit of not watching where my shot goes, especially when I don't hit it well.

We arrived at the green to see three balls scattered around the putting surface, and predictably, my ball was not one of them. I made my way to the back of the green and started searching through the trees and bushes. Nothing. My three friends left their spots on the green and, out of pity, helped me look.

"Did you check the hole?" my friend snickered as he made his way back to the pin.

I wasn't going to satisfy him with a response.

"Brian."

"Shut up."

"Are you (censored) kidding me?"

I looked up. As I did, he yanked the pin out of the hole. My ball popped out with it. A hole in one! I wish I had video evidence of the chaos that ensued as we all celebrated. The worst shot of the day ended up being the best shot of my life. As I replayed the shot and the events leading up to the revelation that my ball somehow found its way into the hole, I thought, *It sure was great my friends could be part of it.*

That led me to another question: What would it have felt like if nobody was there to witness it? Would it still have been great? Sure. But would it have been as great as it was? I don't think so. How would I have experienced that moment if I didn't celebrate it? I was reminded that day that joy is maximized when we can share it with others. That's part of how God designed us. When things happen in isolation, there is a cap on our enjoyment of it. The celebration we had together on the golf course that day helped me understand another way sports can contribute to God's glory and our enjoyment.

> *I was reminded that day that joy is maximized when we can share it with others. That's part of how God designed us.*

Celebration helps complete the highs we experience in sports. C. S. Lewis helped me discover this amazing truth in his book *Reflections on the Psalms* when he wrote, "I think we delight to praise what we enjoy because the praise not merely expresses but completes the enjoyment; it is its appointed consummation. It is not out of compliment that lovers keep on telling one another how beautiful they are; the delight is incomplete till it is expressed."[1]

Imagine accomplishing something great in your sport and not having the opportunity to express it outwardly or have someone to share it with. It would certainly lessen the experience. This is true across all categories of life. It's why we love social media. When something good happens to us, we can hardly hold it in. Sharing becomes an extension of the experience. So we tweet. We post. We snap. We text.

Celebrating good things that happen to us is not evidence of lack of humility; it is part of how God designed us to react. Obviously, when the overflow of our joy takes the form of taunting, a line has been crossed, and the legitimate expression of celebration quickly devolves into a lack of humility. I trust you know the difference between the two. The point is this: our God is a joy optimizer!

So when you experience a victory, don't be afraid to celebrate it. Dance with your teammates, hug your coach, give yourself the permission and freedom to experience the emotion of happiness. (Just be sure to do it with class.) God has given you your gift and sport to glorify him, and one of the ways you can do that is by just enjoying the fun moments your sport brings to you.

Error #2 (from Secular Culture): Money May Not Be Able to Buy You Happiness, but Winning Will

Whether or not he is the greatest quarterback of all time, Tom Brady is at least in the discussion. Apart from his tremendous success on the football field, he has quite a few other things going for him. He's handsome, has a supermodel wife, and has more money than he knows what to do with. Why, then, did he say the following in a 2005 interview with *60 Minutes*?

> Why do I have three Super Bowl rings, and still think there's something greater out there for me? I mean, maybe a lot of people would say, "Hey, man, this is what is." I reached my goal, my dream, my life. Me, I think: God, it's got to be more than this. I mean this can't be what it's all cracked up to be. I mean I've done it. I'm 27. And what else is there for me?[2]

When asked what the answer was, Brady simply responded, "I wish I knew. I wish I knew."

Our culture has no answer for why Brady felt that way. His response goes against everything our culture promises—that we can find happiness in things or experiences. You are not Tom Brady. Your win or success may be simply making the team. Or maybe it's finishing in eighth place but still bettering your personal best by a few seconds. Athlete, you do not need to be at an elite level to live in a destructive cycle that always leaves you wanting more. It's a never-ending cycle that goes something like this. You compete. You win or succeed. It feels good. A short while later, the high is gone, and you need to do it all over again. Sometimes there's outside pressure for you to do it again. Winning gives you a taste of joy, acceptance, and satisfaction, but you want more. This is not surprising to God. He created you in his image, so you are hardwired for more than earthly satisfaction. Sports are wonderful, but they are not the ultimate. They cannot satisfy your heart at the deepest level.

Solomon (or someone an awful lot like him) wrote the book of Ecclesiastes, a book dedicated to lamenting the fact that true joy cannot be found in the pleasures this earth offers. The Bible does not say whether or not King Solomon could throw a baseball or read a zone defense. We do know that he was good looking. He was wise. He was rich. Women loved him. On paper, he had it all. And yet he wrestled with the same issue that Tom Brady and many other athletes wrestle with. Sports can give us some amazing highs, but there's a reason many of us come crashing back down to earth a short while later, and that reason is that we were created for more. We were created for eternity. Winning is great, and we should desire to pursue it, but there is a good reason why it doesn't satisfy us at a soul level. It was never supposed to.

Error #3 (from Christian and Secular Culture): You Should Care More about Trying Your Best Than about Winning

We say this to kids to try to make them feel better when they lose. There's some truth to it, but the bottom line is that in sports, there is almost always a definite winner and a definite loser. That's the point. It's a competition. It is not a bad thing to want to win because that's the purpose of the game. You should want to win. God is not opposed to you playing your sport with excellence.

When you're excellent at what you do, it brings honor to the one who created you and gave you that particular skill set (Prov. 22:29; 1 Cor. 4:7). We often throw around this line: "All God cares about is you giving your best." It has become the consolation prize for losing. It's yet another casualty of our everyone-gets-a-trophy culture. Does God care if you give your best? Absolutely. When athletes give less than their best, they fall short of their calling to steward their gifts to the best of their ability.

The problem with that line is the word *all*. It suggests that God *only* cares about your effort and nothing else. So don't worry if you stink. He's not concerned with your skill level, only how hard you try.

Again, there is an element of truth in that. The problem is that we often limit "giving our best" to our performance on game day. If you are habitually lazy in practice, in the weight room, and with your eating and sleeping habits, and then you give 100 percent during the competition, is that really your best? Does that kind of effort glorify God? Colossians 3:23 encourages us to do everything as if we were doing it for the Lord. That would seem to include the way we prepare for competition.

Imagine if practicing your faith consisted of giving it your all for one hour on Sunday each week. No prayer, no Bible study, and no service the rest of the week. Would that glorify God? Or what if the ark that Noah built was littered with holes? Would God say, "Well, he sure isn't very good at shipbuilding, but I did notice that he was sweating a lot and giving it a good effort." I doubt God would say that.

God didn't merely tell Noah to build a boat. God gave Noah very specific instructions on how to build that boat and expected Noah to follow those instructions with excellence. Providing a detailed set of instructions created the expectation that Noah would follow through, not only with hard work but with excellent work. Effort is not the same as excellence. Read that last sentence again, because we often assume that effort and excellence are one and the same when it comes to glorifying God. But they're not. Both are important and needed, and when combined, they produce a glorifying product.

Athlete, are you becoming excellent at your craft? Are you putting in the necessary preparation and practice time to maximize your abilities? God desires that you give your best effort, but he also wants you to maximize the skill set that he gave you to steward.

Error #4 (from Christian and Secular Culture): Don't Even Think about Praying for a Win

It should come as no surprise that prayer brings glory to God (Phil. 4:19, Acts 10:4, Eph. 3:14). It exalts him as worthy by showing our dependence on him. When we thank God for the opportunity to play or for some success we've enjoyed, we are saying, "What I just experienced was a gift, and I want to recognize you as the giver of that gift."

I once asked a large group of Division I athletes if it was okay for athletes to pray that God would help them win or succeed. Every athlete predictably shook their head no. Regardless of whether or not they had done it, there seemed to be this inherent knowledge that it was wrong to do so. Here's the truth: every athlete wants permission to pray for a win or for a personal best performance.

And I'm ready to give it to you. Yes, go ahead and pray for the win. Pray for your success.

> *Yes, go ahead and pray for the win. Pray for your success.*

Are there better things to pray for besides winning and success? Sure. Nevertheless, when we ask God in prayer to help us win or play well, it gives him glory. Think about it. When you pray, you are acknowledging that you can't do it on your own. You are admitting that you need God's help. When we pray to God for anything or about anything, we are showing our dependence on him and bringing him glory in the process. We show that we are sheep who lack the ability to get what we want without someone to help.

Jesus says in John 15:5, "I am the vine; you are the branches. Whoever abides in me and I in him, he it is that bears much fruit, for apart from me you can do nothing."

Apart from me, you can do nothing.

My two-year-old can't put his shoes on. I get glory not when he sits in the corner and tries to do it himself, but when he carries them over to me, asks for help, and then patiently sits while I put them on for him. I also get glory when he looks up afterward and says, "Thank you!"

Similarly, we glorify God when the prayers we offer up about our sport include thankfulness, praise, and asking.

In a culture that looks up to athletes as gods, prayer becomes a simple way for us to confess this: "You are God, I am not, and I need your help. Thank you." If you want to pray for athletic success, go for it. Keep in mind that God wants you to come to him as you are, not how you think you should be. In other words, he wants honest prayers. At the same time, in coming as you are, you may discover that he changes your desires over time. Herbert McCabe, a priest and theologian, once explained how this works:

> When you pray, consider what you want and need and never mind how vulgar or childish it might appear. If you want very much to pass that exam or get to know that girl or boy better, that is what you should pray for. You could let world peace rest for a while. You may not be ready yet to want that passionately. When you pray you must come before God as honestly as you can. There is no point in pretending to *him*. One of the great human values of prayer is that you face the facts about yourself and admit to what you want; and you know you can talk about this to God because he is totally loving and accepting. In true prayer you must meet God and meet yourself where you really are, for it is just by this that God will move you on from where you really are. For prayer is a bit of a risk. If you pray and acknowledge your most infantile desires, there is every danger that you may grow up a bit, that God will grow you up. When (as honestly as you can) you speak to God of your desires, very gently and tactfully he will often reveal to you that in fact you have deeper and more mature desires. But there is only one way

to find this out: to start from where you are. It is no good pretending to yourself that you are full of high-minded aspirations. You have to wait until you are. If a child is treated as though she were already an adult, she will never become an adult. Prayer is the way in which our Father in heaven leads each of us by different paths to be saints, that is to say, with him.[3]

Now that we have addressed some of the lies about how Christian athletes think about winning, it's time to focus on some positive ways to deal with winning and success that glorify God.

Use the Gifts God Has Given You to Play Your Best and Try to Win the Game

The end goal of a competition is for someone or some team to come out on top. That's why you play the game. There's nothing sinful or evil about that. First Corinthians 9:24 says, "Do you not know that in a race all the runners run, but only one receives the prize? So run that you may obtain it." Now, I realize that Paul is using sports as a metaphor for the Christian life here, but the foundation of the metaphor is that there is a winner and loser in sports. Should a Christian athlete want to win? Yes, that is the point of the game. Does God want a Christian athlete to have a desire to win? Yes, that is the right desire. I would hope that God puts a desire in the heart of a contractor to see a finely built house. I would hope that God puts a desire in the heart of an accountant to see well-prepared, accurate financial statements. I would hope that God puts a desire in the heart of a doctor to correctly diagnose a patient. While there's a sense in which sports are just a game, that doesn't mean they don't matter or that your efforts and desires related to them don't matter. They most certainly do!

God made you with your athletic gifts and gave you a desire for competition for a reason. So try your best to win.

Enjoy the Win but Learn from the Experience

Imagine seeing the Grand Canyon for the first time. Your immediate thought might be, *This is incredible!* That's a natural response. Seeing something amazing should create a sense of awe in you. After all, you were created to enjoy good gifts and the emotions that spring forth when you experience them. Christians have the ability to take these types of experiences and deepen their joy even more.

As a Christian, seeing the Grand Canyon and all its majesty is an opportunity to take your thoughts one step further: *God, you are incredible for creating this! Thank you!* The beauty and majesty of the Grand Canyon triggers worship in a believer. The awe-filled experience leads the Christian to praise God for the awesomeness of his creation. Like my experience with the hole-in-one, having someone to celebrate it with you completes the experience. When we celebrate with God, we not only complete an experience, we maximize it. It might sound a little like this:

"Wow! That is amazing! Thank you, God, for creating it! You are amazing! Thank you for giving me the opportunity to experience this with you!"

The giver of any gift is glorified when the recipient experiences joy and recognizes the giver with thanks.

The giver of any gift is glorified when the recipient experiences joy and recognizes the giver with thanks.

So, athlete, it's good to care about winning and it's good to win. Enjoy your wins and successes. But share those experiences with God. Thank him for the temporary happiness that winning creates. Thank him for the memories you make with teammates and others. In thanking him, acknowledge that he alone can give you ultimate satisfaction.

Humbly Accept Praise

If you win and a reporter or a fan congratulates you, what are you supposed to do? Let's not overcomplicate this. It's not prideful to say thank you for the compliment. It's polite. The reality is that for many of you reading this, a win or success is not going to get you in front of reporters begging for a great quote. What a win does afford you, however, is an opportunity to practice humility and show that while the win was great, God is better still.

In his book *Practicing Affirmation*, Sam Crabtree tells about Corrie ten Boom, who had a unique strategy for graciously handling praise. "When people would honor her, she knew that God was really the one who deserved all the glory and credit, so she would imagine each honor as a huge bouquet of roses. She would picture herself taking in their scent and savoring it for a moment before handing it up to him, the rightful recipient. Smell the roses and hand them up."[4]

So, what are some ways you can celebrate wins with class and humility? One simple way is to shake your opponent's hand after the competition. That's a good application of Philippians 2:4, which says, "Let each of you look not only to his own interests, but also to the interests of others." You should also thank the referees for their service even if you didn't agree with every call. It's also a good practice to encourage your teammates with what they did well during the competition, win or lose.

If you did something in the competition that you regret, you should apologize to the person you offended, whoever it is, whether opponent, official, coach, or teammate. Romans 12:18 says, "If possible, so far as it depends on you, live peaceably with all." There's no need to make enemies before, during, or after the game. Winning doesn't erase any ungodliness that happened during the competition. It's your responsibility as a Christ-follower to take ownership for your part and seek reconciliation. That's what humility is all about. And it is glorifying to God.

CHAPTER 6

ON LOSING

Faithless is he that says farewell when the road darkens.

— Gimli, *The Lord of the Rings*[1]

No competitive athlete enjoys losing, Christian or not. With the amount of time and energy we put into training and preparing, any outcome that does not involve us winning is sure to bring frustration. But we would be wrong to think a losing effort can't bring glory to God. Like the previous chapter on winning, we first need to address some of the poor thinking surrounding the topic of losing before we get into practical advice on how to steward a losing outcome for the glory of God.

Error #1: Don't Be Frustrated When You Lose

The Bible study got away from me. When you lead a Bible study, you need wisdom and discernment to decide when to stay on track and when to follow the rabbit trail the athletes, like you, want to go down. We were not on track. We even veered away from the rabbit trail. Though I had started a study with the cross-country guys on the rich man and Lazarus from Luke 16, I now found myself listening to a long monologue from one of the runners about what it looks like to respond in a godly way when we fail. Wisdom and discernment didn't lead us there; my mind must have wandered for a few minutes as they seized control of the study.

"Take last week," the junior on the team explained. "I was racing the 5k in Iowa and had to drop out. Was I upset? Sure. But I knew that it wasn't right to show that frustration outwardly because everyone was watching. Even God. What kind of Christian would I have been if I had looked overly upset?"

We can correct this lie with the Bible, but we can also use some common sense. If the natural emotion that comes from winning is happiness culminating in celebration, it only makes sense that the natural emotions that follow a loss are frustration and disappointment. When things go wrong, it is okay to feel frustrated and disappointed. You're human, after all. The problem is when your disappointment causes you to sin. Ephesians 4:26 gives us a great life principle that we can use in response to a loss or disappointment in the context of sports: "Be angry and do not sin; do not let the sun go down on your anger." The sin is not in the disappointment we feel, but where the disappointment could potentially lead us. This verse also teaches us to try to limit our frustration (anger) to a particular period of time and not let it go on indefinitely. Specifically, it says that we should not go to bed angry. The context of the verse relates to interpersonal relationships, but hanging onto anger about anything will at the very least interrupt your sleep, and at the worst lead to bitterness and a whole host of other sins.

What are some of these sins? In his book *Game Day for the Glory of God*, Stephen Altrogge gives three temptations following a loss: we can be quick to criticize others, agonize over the defeat, and succumb to feelings of shame.[2] I would add to the list that we can become short with our coaches, teammates, opponents, and fans. Basically, we can become irritable, self-absorbed, and discouraged. Athlete, you have permission to be upset personally, but just be careful it does not cause you to lash out relationally.

Error #2: You Have Less of an Impact for God When You Lose

After God used Moses to lead his people out of slavery in Egypt and on a path to the Promised Land, he gave Moses a set of laws for the people to follow. In addition to aligning themselves with the character and purposes of God, these laws also set the Israelites apart from other nations. Deuteronomy 4:5–6 explains it this way:

> See, I have taught you statutes and rules, as the LORD my God commanded me, that you should do them in the land that you are entering to take possession of it. Keep them and do them, for that will be your wisdom and your understanding in the sight of the peoples, who, when they hear all these statutes, will say, "Surely this great nation is a wise and understanding people."

God gave them laws and told them how to act so they would stand out and be different from the surrounding nations. The idea was that other nations would take notice and say, "Wow! Look how different they are from everyone else." And then they would ask, "What is it about them that causes them to act the way they do?" They were meant to be a peculiar people, a light to the nations. (Of course, they ultimately failed in their calling, and Christ accomplished what they couldn't.)

I'm not making a direct comparison between today's athlete and the Israelites. But there is a principle here to understand. When God's people look different from the rest of culture, culture tends to notice. This theme is seen in the New Testament and throughout the history of the church. God's people are called to practice obedience in the midst of trying circumstances. When they do, people notice. Culture changes. Movements of justice and human flourishing rise up. As we've said, looking different doesn't mean pretending you're not disappointed. When you lose, it's okay to feel some frustration and disappointment. The line is crossed, however, when those emotions cause you to sin.

When a Christian athlete wins, people expect him or her to give some of the credit to God. What culture doesn't expect is for you to acknowledge God even when you lose. Athlete, your struggles on the playing field do not minimize your platform for Christ. In fact, it may be even greater following a loss. A loss can be an opportunity to shatter the cultural expectation.

Something I've noticed from working in sports ministry is that when Christian athletes win and use their platform to talk about Jesus, Christians notice and want to hear more from that athlete. When Christian athletes lose and still make much of Jesus, non-Christians see and want to know more from that athlete. Anyone can talk about how awesome Jesus is on the heels of a win or outstanding performance. Our culture's idea of happiness is attached to the blessings we experience in life. That's why losing affords us an opportunity to show that our joy in Christ transcends outward circumstances. So stand out from the crowd in the midst of a tough loss. Feel the freedom to be a Christian athlete and be disappointed at the outcome of a competition, but rebound

Athletic success may build the platform that gets you noticed, but how you respond to a loss might be what allows you to capitalize on it for the glory of God.

quickly and don't let any residual negative emotions lead you to being a jerk. Simply maintaining perspective can be a powerful witness. Athletic success may build the platform that gets you noticed, but how you respond to a loss might be what allows you to capitalize on it for the glory of God.

Here are a few ways you can look different outwardly:

- Thank God for the opportunity to compete.
- Lead both teams in prayer after the competition.
- Shake your opponent's hand.
- Encourage your teammates with encouraging words.
- Thank the referees or officials.
- Leverage social media in a genuine way that shows you have perspective on the loss.

Athlete, God is glorified when we look different than everyone else. Don't waste your losses.

Error #3: If You Are Disobedient in Your Personal Life, God Is Less Likely to Bless You with a Win

If you lost, it's not because you didn't pray hard enough or sinned earlier in the week, or because you didn't have enough faith. To believe that would mean you would have won if you had done the right things. God cannot be manipulated that way.

I once discipled an athlete who was convinced God had promised him success. The promises were specific: NCAA Championship. MVP. First pick overall. Even the team that would eventually draft him. When none of those came true, he had to choose one of three reasons:

1. He heard incorrectly.
2. God lied to him.
3. He didn't have enough faith.

He chose number three. He opted to believe that God had great things in store for him, but first, he had to hold up his end of the bargain. He needed to be obedient in all situations or God would take back his promises. He needed to believe with all his heart, leaving no room for a sliver of doubt, or God would withhold those promises. He was trying to manipulate God into getting what he wanted.

We've all done it before. Some of us may still do it. We have used God as a rabbit's foot or a good luck charm for our personal gain, win, or power. We understand we don't deserve free gifts, so we try to behave better. We work as hard as we can to refrain from sin in the days (or hours) leading up to competition, and then we pray that God will bless us for being so amazing. It would be funny if it weren't true. But the fact that it's true is what makes it so tragic.

The beauty of the gospel is that God does not bless us based on our awesomeness, but on his. Second Corinthians 5:21 says, "For our sake he made him to be sin who knew no sin, so that in him we might become the righteousness of God." We don't need to perform for God in order for him to bless us. Jesus already performed for us.

For many of us, the danger isn't in trusting him for big things he never promised in the first place, but in thinking he will reward athletic success with obedience or withhold it when we become disobedient. Our obedience should be birthed out of a desire to please our heavenly Father, not out of a misguided belief that our goodness can be exchanged for an earthly blessing like athletic success. God is not a genie. He is not a lucky rabbit's foot. He is King. He is Savior. He is Father. Ask what you want of him on the basis of who he is, not who you are.

How can we handle losing better and respond to a loss in a way that glorifies God? Three things come to mind.

Confess

Can we be honest here? Most, if not all of us, will respond to a loss in a sinful way, whether through outward actions or inward thoughts. Sometimes the simplest way to glorify God is through confessing your sin to him. Here's a prayer that I have prayed many times: "God forgive me for my actions following the loss today. I placed more value on the outcome of a game than I did in my allegiance to you. Forgive my inappropriate fixation on both my failure and success in the midst of competition that I reject the grace you freely offer me to move forward. Help me to find contentment in you, not in the outcome of a game. Give me the grace to do better next time."

Have Perspective

Maintaining perspective is key. Here's some mic-dropping truth from Stephen Altrogge:

> No matter how significant they may seem, all our wins and losses are insignificant in the grand scheme of things. There are no lives hanging in the balance, nor is the peace of the free world dependent on whether we win or lose. God's kingdom will continue to advance even if our softball team doesn't.[3]

At the end of the day, it's a game you're playing. Your internal and external response should reflect that reality. As we've said, it's understandable that you'd be upset in the moments after a loss. However, a Christian athlete's mourning period following a loss should be pretty short. Real tragedy comes not only when we lose the game but when we lose focus on what God prioritizes: our heart's response to adversity.

Real tragedy comes not only when we lose the game but when we lose focus on what God prioritizes: our heart's response to adversity.

If we want to have a proper perspective on losing and respond in a way that pleases God and brings us contentment, we need to pay attention to what's going on in our hearts following a loss. Here are some good questions to ask yourself after a losing effort:

- Do I have sinful anger in my heart over the loss, or am I simply a little frustrated that I put in so much hard work and fell short this time?
- Are what-if questions consuming my thought life?
- Am I thinking poorly of my teammates or coaches because of what happened?
- Am I acting like Jesus would toward my teammates, opponents, coaches, and refs following the game?

Look for the Wins

I grew up playing every sport imaginable. For someone who would eventually run track and cross country, I was actually a pretty coordinated athlete (if you have ever seen a runner try to play a sport that involves a ball, you know what I'm talking about). But coordination means very little when you enter high school at 4'10" and 95 lbs. My small stature—and the fact that I was just not as good as I thought I was—led me to getting cut from three sports my first three weeks as a freshman. I was devastated. But God had a bigger win in mind through what were at the time some of the bigger losses in my life. My youth pastor tells the story better than I could:

> Josh burst into my office with a freshman guy named Brian. It seems Brian had been cut from the team. For the third time. Three sports in a row— whack, whack, whack. That had to be a record at our school. Most kids sank into depression after one cut. But three? So there they stood in front of me. Before I could say anything Josh got in my face and announced, "Me and Brian are starting

our own basketball league and we need the church gym. You got a problem with that?"...Now a decade later, Josh has a good job, a wonderful wife, and kids of his own. And this year he's helping oversee the basketball league he and Brian started. You see, their league not only survived—it's become a legend in our area. In its tenth season at this writing, the Blythefield Basketball Association (BBA) is student-led, supports 280 players on 28 teams, and features a website, employees, refs, draft day, trades, a full set of stats, and cell-phone-toting agents. What's more, students share the gospel over one hundred times each year during halftime at these games. As a result, thousands have been introduced to Christ, many join small groups, and sometimes entire families land in church."[4]

Let me give you another example of how God has used a loss to give me something better than a win ever could. Eventually I ended up on the cross country team because it was one of the only sports you can't get cut from. After working hard for three years, things started to click for me, and my times dropped significantly. The fall of my junior year, our team was one of the top-ranked cross country programs in the entire United States. We were good. Really good. Winning the state meet should have been a formality, but something happened. With a mile to go, my body stopped working, and I collapsed into a crowd of screaming fans. Ten minutes later, I found myself in a medical tent with IVs in both arms and my parents by my side. My coach stopped by to check on me—or to just tell me the news. We lost. I cost my team a state title that, up to this point, our school had never won. Again, I was devastated. As I sat up in the bed, one of the girls on the team popped her head in the tent and asked if I was okay. She asked if she could pray for me. And she did. We had never really talked up to this point because of the size of our cross-country program, but mostly because she was way out of my league. But Linsey Blaisdell was drawn to people in need. And this was about as needy as I could get.

Her name is now Linsey Smith, and we have three kids. We started dating a few months after my dreadful state meet "performance" and have literally been together ever since—all because I lost the state meet for our team. At the time, I would have given anything to stand on that podium. Knowing how God used the result, however, I would suffer that loss a thousand times over. God used the biggest loss of my life to give me what has been my greatest blessing.

Often, losing feels like a step back, a missed opportunity. It's hard to see how anything good could come from a loss. We would do well to remember that God often works in ways that are different from what we would expect. Isaiah 55:8 reminds us that our thoughts fail to align with his thoughts, and our ways of doing things are different than his. In light of that truth, we need to ask this question: What opportunities does losing provide? That requires us to pay attention to what is going on around us because of a losing effort. Even if the door to winning slammed shut, what other doors could God be opening?

Remember, your sport is a vehicle to help you love and serve God and others. It's not just for you. We can't make a deal with God that our obedience must be rewarded with wins. God has shown us that his blueprint for expanding his kingdom often involves seemingly backward methods. He asked Abraham to sacrifice his own son, a son through whom God said he would bless all nations. He asked Gideon to substantially reduce the

God has shown us that his blueprint for expanding his kingdom often involves seemingly backward methods.

number of people in his army before going on the offensive. He told Joshua to walk around Jericho for a week blowing trumpets instead of attacking the walls using conventional methods of war. He took everything from Job instead of rewarding him for his obedience. He sent his one and only Son to die in our place. Get the point? Just because things didn't work out the way you wanted or expected doesn't mean God isn't up to something good. Ask him what he is doing, and express an openness to join him in it.

A brief word of caution before moving on. By his grace, God allowed me to see the good that came out of a couple of horrible losses in my life. One of those took a year to see, the other took about six years. I've had other losses about which I still wonder what God is or was doing in allowing them. The point is that we are not entitled to know. Maybe God will show us. Maybe he won't. But I have to believe he wants us to trust that he is up to something good, even when the scoreboard doesn't fall in our favor.

Get Better

You never know what's in a sponge until you squeeze it. You can make some assumptions about what's inside, but until you compress it, you won't really know. God can use our losses as a sponge to bring some of the nastiness inside of us out into the light. And that is a loving thing for him to do. For us to be molded into the likeness of Jesus, we need to know what needs molding. James 1:2–4 takes it to another level when it says, "Count it all joy, my brothers, when you meet trials of various kinds, for you know that the testing of your faith produces steadfastness. And let steadfastness have its full effect, that you may be perfect and complete, lacking in nothing."

What do you notice about your attitude or your actions after a loss? Does it reveal entitlement? Anger? Bitterness? A complaining spirit? A tendency to shift the blame? Losing gives you an opportunity to look in the mirror at your response and see where you need to change. While losing a competition amounts to an earthly loss, it can help you win huge spiritual gains.

Athlete, don't waste your losing efforts. Continue to put your hope in God. Trust him with the unknown. Show by your attitude that he is enough and confess where you have fallen short. Commit to changing the revealed weaknesses he shows you. And finally, take the wise advice of Dr. Seuss (which conveniently aligns with the biblical truth of Philippians 3:12–16): "When something bad happens, you have three choices. You can either let it define you, let it destroy you, or you can let it strengthen you."[5]

Chapter 7

ON INJURIES

The most painful times in our lives are times in which... our idols are being threatened or removed.

—Tim Keller

When I understand that everything happening to me is to make me more Christlike, it resolves a great deal of anxiety.

—A. W. Tozer

Injuries are awful. Anybody who has played sports has had to deal with them to some extent. (If you haven't, count your blessings but know they are usually part of the deal.) While there is physical pain associated with an injury, there are other, greater factors that contribute to their awfulness.

Injuries inhibit us from playing at 100 percent and rob us of the optimal level of performance we work so hard to reach. Injuries can halt any momentum we may have gained in our training. They can sideline us not only from competition but also from our community as we now spend our practice time on the training table instead of with our teammates. Injuries can even leave us with a lot of uncertainty about our future in the sport.

An injury can cause us to ask questions like these: Will I get better? If I do recover, will I return to peak form or merely be a hobbled version of my former self? Will I be able to play without fear, or will I always be a little cautious? When I return, will I still have my spot, or will a teammate step in and grab it?

Despite the validity of questions like these, for the Christian athlete, the biggest question tends to be this: Why would God allow something like this to happen? As we have done with other topics, we want to look at how we can use an injury (and the circumstances surrounding the injury) to deepen our relationship with God and glorify him through it.

It starts with being honest with him.

I remember sitting down with a guy I was discipling who played defensive tackle for a D1 football team. He was a senior. It was early in the college football season, and his name was already showing up in mock drafts on the Internet (a mock draft is an effort to guess where top-ranked players will go in the upcoming NFL draft). He was going to live out his dream of playing in the NFL, as long as he stayed healthy. As he was chasing down an opposing player, his knee twisted, and he fell to the ground. He tore his MCL. His future was now uncertain, yet when I met with him, he tried to stay positive.

"I know God's got me," he said.

"Are you frustrated? Have you told him how you feel? He can handle it, you know. Be honest with him. Don't treat him like the media and give rehearsed lines that sound good but don't reflect how you feel," I pressed. I could see tears starting to well up in his eyes.

He came back the next week a changed man. His MCL didn't miraculously heal. He still faced a lot of uncertainty. But he was honest with God about his frustrations and felt the freedom to cry out to him in anger and disappointment. In doing so, he began a process that every Christian athlete needs to wrestle with if he or she wants to leverage an injury to glorify God.

Dr. Henry Cloud points out in his book *Changes That Heal*, "Real intimacy always comes in the company of truth."[1] Relationships are healthy and grow when honesty is present. God can handle our honesty. He has a big enough chest for us to pound on it from time to time.

He Can Handle It

King David in the Bible models well for us what it looks like to come before God without polished religious phrases. He approached God in prayer with a rawness that I envy. Here are a few examples from the Psalms where David cried out to God with brutal honesty:

> I cried aloud (3:4).
> I was in distress (4:1).
> Consider my groaning (5:1).
> I am languishing (6:2).
> My bones are troubled (6:2).
> My soul also is greatly troubled (6:3).
> I am weary with my moaning (6:6).
> I flood my bed with tears (6:6).
> See my affliction (9:13).
> How long must I...have sorrow in my heart all the day? (13:2).

I find no rest (22:2).
I am lonely and afflicted (25:16).
The troubles of my heart are enlarged (25:17).

The prophet Jeremiah cried out to God, "O Lord, you have deceived me, and I was deceived; you are stronger than I, and you have prevailed. I have become a laughingstock all the day; everyone mocks me" (Jer. 20:7).

That is bold. But God can handle it.

Perhaps we have no greater example of what it looks like to come before God with raw honesty than Jesus himself. Before he was betrayed by Judas and went to the cross, he prayed the same prayer three times to the Father: "My Father, if it be possible, let this cup pass from me; nevertheless, not as I will, but as you will" (Matt. 26:39). Jesus knew the plan, was anxious about it, and was honest before God about how he was feeling in that moment.

God Already Knows Anyway

The second reason we should be honest with God is that he already knows what we are feeling. Listen, again, to the prophet Jeremiah: "O Lord of hosts, who tests the righteous, who sees the heart and the mind, let me see your vengeance upon them, for to you have I committed my cause" (Jer. 20:12). Jeremiah plainly says that God sees the mind and the heart. He knows what we are thinking.

Along the same lines, Jesus, on multiple occasions, perceived the thoughts of those around him (Matt. 9:4, 22:18; Mark 2:8; Luke 6:8; Luke 11:17).

Have you ever played hide and seek with a little kid? If you have, you know they are awful at the game. They usually hide in the same place you hid when it was your turn, and when they try someplace new, they usually end up curled in a ball in the middle of the room with their eyes closed and a blanket over the top of them.

Trying to hide our real emotions from God is like playing hide and seek with him. We are the unimaginative kids who hide in plain sight. It's a futile game to play with an all-knowing God. Be honest with God about what you are feeling when you're injured. He already knows how you feel, and he can handle it. And it will help you deal with the injury when you include him in the process.

Get Perspective

After we are honest with God, we need to gain some perspective. Perspective on injuries is a little like Advil—it's not going to heal us, but it makes the pain a bit more manageable. Having perspective also opens the door for us to hope. When we know God has a plan, even if we are not thrilled about it, we open ourselves up to the idea that God is telling a bigger story than our current circumstances allow us to see. Why would God allow you to get injured? Here are a few possible reasons.

Perspective on injuries is a little like Advil—it's not going to heal us, but it makes the pain a bit more manageable.

- He is preparing you for something in the future.
- He wants you to deal with something in the present.
- He wants to use you to reach someone.

He Is Preparing You for Something in the Future

Perhaps God is using the circumstance of your injury to prepare you for something in the future.[2] The Bible has no shortage of examples of God's people going through seemingly insignificant circumstances only to later discover that those very circumstances played a vital role in shaping their readiness for future opportunities.

Joseph exemplifies a man who refused to be defined by his circumstances. His brothers sold him into slavery because they were jealous of him, and then Potiphar threw him into prison on a faulty rape charge. He could have easily lived in bitterness and self-pity. Instead, he chose to remain faithful to the Lord. While in prison, Joseph interpreted the dreams of two fellow inmates as well as Pharaoh's. Pharaoh was impressed. He elevated Joseph to second in command of all of Egypt. Joseph leveraged his new position of authority to prepare the nation of Egypt—and his family—for the coming famine. His position and wisdom in preparation saved everyone.

Let's also look at David. When Samuel came to Jesse's house to find the next king of Israel, Jesse brought out his sons for examination. There was only one problem. He forgot David. Often overlooked as the youngest of the brothers, David spent years riding the bench. While his brothers were off at battle, David was shepherding the family's sheep and working on his slingshot skills. When Goliath challenged any man in Israel to a one-on-one battle, David was ready. With one accurately placed shot, he took down Goliath and claimed victory for God's people.

Tamar's husband died. Her dead husband's brother was supposed to marry her. He died, too. Judah, her father-in-law, promised to give her his third son. He didn't. We later read that Judah saw a woman on the side of the road and thought she was a prostitute and slept with her. The woman turned out to be— you guessed it: Tamar. She would have twins as a result of this incestuous one-day stand. One of the boys was named Perez. We read in Matthew's genealogy of Jesus Christ that he (Jesus) came from the lineage of Perez.

Athlete, you never know what God could have in store for you in the future. Trust that he sees you in your present circumstances. Trust that he is in control. And trust the he is good.

He Wants You to Deal with Something in the Present

Pastor Matt Chandler once said, "God is not the ambulance driver that shows up after the wreck. He's the surgeon that will make the cut, knowing exactly what to cut out, exactly what to leave in, exactly what to take, exactly what to let alone. This is the giant, scary, worthy of worship, eternal God of the Bible, who not only knows tomorrow but is already there."[3]

This is a scary truth to wrestle with. God loves us so much that sometimes he acts as a surgeon and proactively removes the problem before it causes us greater harm. Perhaps your injury is God putting you on the sideline because something is going on inside of you that you refuse to address. Maybe, in his love, he is taking away the distraction of your sport to force you to deal with it. It wouldn't be the first time God has done something like that.

Jonah is an interesting guy. We know he's a prophet. So on some level, he can be God's mouthpiece for the people. His job is pretty simple. Hear from God and share it with the people. But God knows there is some pruning that needs to happen in Jonah's heart, so he gives Jonah an assignment: tell the people of Nineveh to repent. Jonah tries to run away and not deal with the issue, so God steps in and, like a masterful surgeon, gets Jonah swallowed up by a large fish. Jonah repents, goes to Nineveh, and shares God's message with them.

Sometimes we are so distracted by what is happening with our sport that we are unaware of the dangerous trajectory our heart is on.

The entire city of Nineveh repents, and God spares them—and Jonah is furious. He didn't want God to save those "wicked" people. God knew that there was pride growing in the heart of Jonah, so he forced Jonah to confront it.

Sometimes we are so distracted by what is happening with our sport that we are unaware of the dangerous trajectory our heart is on. God may be using an injury to force you to deal with an issue in your life that you are currently ignoring because you are so preoccupied with your athletic career.

He Wants to Use You to Reach Someone

Second Corinthians 5:17–20 shines a light on an incredible truth:

> Therefore, if anyone is in Christ, he is a new creation. The old has passed away; behold, the new has come. All this is from God, who through Christ reconciled us to himself and gave us the ministry of reconciliation; that is, in Christ God was reconciling the world to himself, not counting their trespasses against them, and entrusting to us the message of reconciliation. Therefore, we are ambassadors for Christ, God making his appeal through us. We implore you on behalf of Christ, be reconciled to God.

Translation: Once you become a Christian, you become a missionary.

Whether you consider yourself a missionary or not doesn't matter. God considers you one, and his opinion will always trump yours. We have been given the "ministry of reconciliation" and are "Christ's ambassadors." We have a north star, a life's purpose.

Why must we understand this? Because while a sport may be an important pursuit for a Christian, it is not his or her primary objective. Our primary objective, as Christians, is to love God and love others (Matt. 22:36–39). An overflow of this purpose becomes sharing God's message of love, grace, and forgiveness with the people around us.

Your responsibility as a Christian who happens to be an athlete is to consistently ask yourself this question: Who might God want me to reach where I am right now?

Injuries force you to stop your normal rhythms. Your schedule looks different. The places where you spend your time are different. And the people you spend time with are different. Doctors. Nurses. Trainers. Injured teammates. Injured athletes who are not a part of your team. The new network of people you spend time with becomes the new scope of your mission field.

Athlete, God may have you injured at this particular moment because it forces you to spend time with someone who desperately needs to hear about the love he freely offers through Christ. And God has granted you the privilege to be the one who tells this person. It certainly would not be the first time God has used tough circumstances as a means to relocate his people for the advancement of the gospel.

In Acts 16:22–34, Paul and Silas were stripped down, severely beaten, and thrown in jail. That same night, there was a violent earthquake that shook the prison and loosened the chains of the prisoners. Paul and Silas were free. But they didn't flee. They knew they were not in that prison by accident. There was a purpose in their present pain. They ended up sharing the good news of Jesus with the jailer, and he was saved that very night. The possible ripple effects of his conversion are fun to imagine. As Christians around the city would continue to be persecuted and thrown into jail, this jailer may have been the person who watched over them, cared for them, and encouraged them. Only the Lord knows the good that flowed out of this man's life because of the awareness and faithfulness of Paul and Silas to seize the opportunity to share their faith.

Maybe you are injured for a similar reason. That doctor, nurse, trainer, or student-trainer is in a unique position to serve and care for athletes. What if their future care consisted not only of meeting physical needs but spiritual needs as well? The ripple effects could be far greater than we can imagine.

We Want to Be the Hero

There is one other thing worth mentioning. It may be hard to hear. You are not entitled to know what the purpose of your injury is or what good will come from it. It could be that the ripple effects of your injury are part of God's plan in ways that have no direct impact on you. Even so, you can be sure there is a purpose in everything and every situation. Perhaps your injury served the purpose of God doing something in the life of your teammate who took your spot.

Early on in the Old Testament, Moses gets a lot of press. Sure, he has his flaws, including being a stuttering, insecure murderer, but that doesn't stop God from using him. What becomes easy to miss, however, is the fact that for 400 years, the Israelites suffered at the hands of their slavemasters. As my pastor likes to point out, "They made bricks and died." For 400 years. These Israelites were a mere footnote in history. As athletes, most of us want to be the hero at some level. Even in the midst of an injury, we want to be able to point to the reason and purpose behind it. We cry out to God, "Just tell me my role, and I will try to be as faithful as I can." Sometimes we are more like Moses, playing a central role in what's going on around us. Other times, we play the role of the Israelites, seemingly forgotten, unimportant, a footnote in a bigger story.

Regardless of what is going on, know that there is purpose in your pain. To be the best possible steward of your circumstances, including an injury, you need to trust God and open your eyes and heart to his greater purposes rather than sit in self-pity. You need to be okay with the possibility that God may be up to something that has more to do with someone else than with you. Your injuries will always be an opportunity to glorify God through trusting that he is in control and working all things together for your good—even if his idea of what's good doesn't initially align with yours.

CHAPTER 8

ON PRACTICE

*To have love as the guiding principle of our lives
means that our continual mindset in all we do should
be "What will serve the other person?"
It is not "What will serve me?"*

— Matt Perman

What is practice? The *Merriam-Webster Dictionary* defines it this way: "to perform or work at repeatedly so as to become proficient."

Practice is more than an opportunity to get better. The Christian athlete's definition of practice must expand past the boundaries our world places around it. A serious athlete will spend anywhere from 20 to 40 hours a week at practice. That's a lot of time to devote to getting better at a sport. God has some other things going on while we are at practice that need our attention.

If there was ever a place within athletics that we need to apply some new, unfamiliar, and potentially uncomfortable concepts, it's practice. How should a Christian athlete approach this often ignored aspect of competing in a sport?

Practice Is about More Than You

Practice: to perform or work at repeatedly so as to become proficient. Who is doing the practicing? You are. You perform. You work. You repeat. You become proficient. You. You. You.

The very definition of practice assumes you are the subject. No wonder it is so easy for us to get this one backward. In today's culture, practice is about you putting in the time and effort to get better.

For the Christian athlete, practice should primarily be about others, not yourself. It's an opportunity to show respect to your coaches by doing what they say, working hard, and showing humility. It's an opportunity to deepen relationships with your teammates.

Do a quick Google search of *selflessness* and *happiness*. You'll find study after study concluding that having a mindset centered on others will lead you to experience the maximum amount of joy. Many of these studies claim to have unlocked a secret that has actually been hidden in plain sight. God has been telling us this from the beginning.

Galatians 6:2: "Bear one another's burdens, and so fulfill the law of Christ."

Hebrews 6:10: "For God is not unjust so as to overlook your work and the love that you have shown for his name in serving the saints, as you still do."

Hebrews 13:16: "Do not neglect to do good and to share what you have, for such sacrifices are pleasing to God."

John 15:12–13: "This is my commandment, that you love one another as I have loved you. Greater love has no one than this, that someone lay down his life for his friends."

Matthew 5:42: "Give to the one who begs from you, and do not refuse the one who would borrow from you."

Philippians 2:3–4: "Do nothing from selfish ambition or conceit, but in humility count others more significant than yourselves. Let each of you look not only to his own interests, but also to the interests of others."

Romans 15:1: "We who are strong have an obligation to bear with the failings of the weak, and not to please ourselves."

Is practice an opportunity to get better as an athlete? Absolutely. We glorify God when we give it our best (Col. 3:17). We must not neglect the desire to improve, but that motivation must be secondary. This sounds crazy, I know.

This is a major perspective shift that will only take a few minor adjustments.

Before you leave the locker room, make it a point to find a teammate and ask if they are ready to go. Doing so builds a habit into your workout to think of someone else besides yourself.

After the workout, compliment one of your teammates for something they did well. When we see something commendable in others, whether in attitude or action, the Christian thing to do is point it out and praise it. Anything that even remotely mirrors one of Jesus's many excellences is deserving of affirmation.

Simple enough? The real challenge will be incorporating this others-centered mindset during the workout itself. Again, this takes only a few minor adjustments to your habits.

Remember the concept of having a focal point to serve as motivation? A focal point is something you can quickly concentrate on that realigns your focus to your ultimate motivation for playing your sport: glorifying God. You can— and should—have more than one focal point. Each one will serve as a different reminder. So pick a practice focal point. The purpose of this visible reminder in practice will be to help to realign your focus from yourself to others. When you see that focal point, ask yourself this simple question: Who could use a word of encouragement right now? It is a question, but it is also a prayer to God. "God, who needs you at this moment? How can I communicate your love through a simple word of encouragement?"

The Christian athlete is called to put others first. Practice is a great opportunity to...practice this.

Practice Is about More Than Proficiency

The purpose of practice is to become proficient. Repeated actions lead us to the end goal of proficiency. And yet, for the Christian athlete, the purpose of practice transcends proficiency. The purpose of practice is ultimately to glorify God. What does that mean? As we learned in Chapter 1, we give glory to God as athletes when we think and act in a way that pleases him and draws attention to who he is. How do you do that in practice? Simply by practicing at a high level.

Colossians 3:23 says, "Whatever you do, work heartily, as for the Lord and not for men." This verse covers it all for the athlete. What kind of effort should you give? You should work hard. Who should you do it for? For the Lord. Who shouldn't you do it for? People, which is to say your teammates, coaches, fans, and anyone else. And when should you do all of this? Anytime you do anything, sports included.

Your motivation in practice should be to engage in it as if you were doing it for the Lord. The Christian athlete should be the hardest working athlete on earth because he or she is playing for an audience of One. What does this look like practically? Show up early. Stay late. Get in extra reps. Run an extra mile. Get in an extra lift session. Get additional treatment. By separating yourself from the pack with your work ethic, your teammates and coaches will get a small glimpse of the God you serve, an incredible byproduct of playing for an audience of One.

As God's ambassador, you have been given the opportunity to represent God to your teammates and coaches. How hard you work, your energy level, your attitude, all reflect back on the God you serve. Practice becomes a key environment for influencing others for God.

Competition is the arena where you stand out in front of the fans and the community.

Competing like a beast will win you the respect of the outsiders watching you. But practicing like a beast will win you the respect of your teammates and coaches.

Practice Is about More Than Repitition

If you were to picture what practice looks like right now, you would most likely imagine yourself in action—performing, working, and repeating to get better. That's a big part of it, but we do ourselves a disservice when we limit practice to the field, track, pool, or court. When we relegate practice to the workout, we are in danger of missing out on one of the greatest blessings that comes with our sport: the relationships we form.

For the Christian athlete, practice is more than actions we perform. Practice includes the drive, walk, or bike to the locker room. Practice includes the locker room banter among your teammates. Practice includes the cool-down and the stretching. Practice includes the ice baths and the treatment. Practice includes the shower and getting ready to go. And practice includes the drive, walk, or bike back to your dorm, house, or apartment. So it's not just the reps that matter; it's the whole process from beginning to end.

Why is it so important to widen our view of what practice is and when it takes place? As a Christian, it's vital for us to see how practice becomes one of the primary avenues that God gives us to build relationships. When we widen our parameters for what practice includes, we begin to see it as more than just preparation for the next competition. It becomes one of the primary places where relationships form and grow.

Through competition, you will remember the performance.

Through practice, you will remember the people.

> *Through competition, you will remember the performance. Through practice, you will remember the people.*

Relationships will always have more lasting value and joy than the trophies we earn. When we place a higher emphasis on the award, we are valuing the praise of people—which the trophy brings—over the friendship of people. That's a bad trade. Again, this is a major perspective shift that will only take a few minor adjustments. Here are a few of ways to have a more holistic view of practice.

- Don't travel alone. Go to and from the workout with a teammate.
- Don't zone out. Put the headphones down and engage with your teammates before the workout starts and after it ends.
- Don't just be an ambassador for Christ during the workout. Be an ambassador in the locker room, too. Ephesians 5:4 says "Let there be no filthiness nor foolish talk nor crude joking, which are out of place, but instead let there be thanksgiving." Acting like that might make you stand out among your teammates, which is the point, and if you're consistent and don't come across as judgmental or holier-than-thou, they will usually respect how you conduct yourself.

Practice Is about More Than Work

Most athletes dread practice. To classify it as work is probably an understatement. Athletes endure practice because of the hope that it can, and will, produce long-term benefits. They see it as a necessary means to an end. The harder you work your muscles, the stronger they become. The joy comes from the competition—or rather the result of the competition—not the repetition experienced in practice.

At some level, every athlete will have a strained relationship with practice. For the Christian athlete, there needs to be an appreciation for how God has designed the body to function. I am not talking about the ability of muscles to get stronger, which is reason enough to appreciate God's design, but something deeper that God offers to everyone.

God has designed our bodies in such a way that when we exercise, we actually experience happiness. How does this work? When you start working out, your brain interprets this as stress.[1] When your heart rate increases, your brain believes you are either fighting someone or fleeing from someone. As a way to protect yourself and your brain from this stress, your body releases a protein called BDNF (brain-derived neurotrophic factor). If you ever wonder why you often feel at ease and have an added sense of clarity and happiness after working out, you can thank BDNF. It has a protective and also reparative effect on your memory neurons and acts as a reset switch.

While your brain releases BDNF, it also releases endorphins, other chemicals to fight stress. Researcher M. K. McGovern describes some of the benefits of endorphins: "These endorphins tend to minimize the discomfort of exercise and are even associated with a feeling of euphoria."[2]

God's creative design enables the release of BDNF and endorphins during exercise, giving us the ability to feel good in moments of discomfort. John Piper wrote of these positive effects in *When I Don't Desire God*: "Either brief periods of intense training or prolonged aerobic workouts raise levels of chemicals in the brain, such as endorphins, adrenaline, serotonin, and dopamine, that produce feelings of pleasure."[3]

Athlete, the same God that designed sex to be pleasurable created the chemical balance of our bodies to respond in such a way that when you train, it ultimately brings you good feelings.

Is practice tough? Absolutely. But come to practice with an expectation that God is going to use physical exercise to increase your joy at that moment. You may be dreading going to practice today, but it could be the very thing that enables you to enjoy the rest of your day. God designed it that way and is glorified when the process works as he intended it.

It has been said that there is no glory in practice, but without practice, there is no glory. It's true. For the athlete trying to gain glory, practice becomes merely a means to an end. For the Christian athlete, however, practice serves a greater purpose. For the Christian athlete, practice is not about gaining glory at all; it's about giving glory.

CHAPTER 9

ON TEAMMATES

How you treat people reveals what you believe about God.

—Jackie Hill Perry

Johnny was in a great spot. He was well liked and really skilled at whatever he did. Along with being outstanding, he had the additional benefit of knowing the position was guaranteed to be his. He was literally born to do this. You can imagine his shock when he found out it was given to someone else before he even had a chance to prove himself.

This has nothing to do with sports. Johnny was a biblical character referred to as Jonathan. His dad, Saul, was the King of Israel. As his son, Jonathan was the rightful heir to the throne. But don't imagine him as some stuck-up rich kid. Jonathan was very capable. He would have been a great king but wasn't given the opportunity. Rather than complain, Jonathan chose to make the best of the situation. And because of his unselfish attitude, he became one of the greatest teammates this world has ever known. He is a model of a gospel-centered teammate.

Gospel-Centered Teammates Have Ambition

> One day Jonathan the son of Saul said to the young man who carried his armor, "Come, let us go over to the Philistine garrison on the other side." But he did not tell his father" (1 Sam. 14:1).

Before David arrives on the scene, we catch a glimpse of the character and ambition of Jonathan. As the son of King Saul, Jonathan has the right to the throne after his father's reign is over. He doesn't have to prove anything. The spot is his. We see that he isn't satisfied with playing it safe, however. Without his father's knowledge—or permission—Jonathan sets a plan in motion to conquer the Philistines.

Great teammates are not passive. They have a personal ambition to be the best they can be. Even if they are the frontrunners for "the spot" on the team, they don't take it for granted.

Gospel-Centered Teammates Learn from Other Great Teammates

> And his armor-bearer said to him, "Do all that is in your heart. Do as you wish. Behold, I am with you heart and soul" (1 Sam. 14:7).

After Jonathan shares the plan, his armor-bearer, the only other person to go along with him, has his back. He puts Jonathan's interests above his own. There is a huge difference between "I support you" and "I am with you heart and soul." They are going to succeed together or die together trying. His armor-bearer was a great teammate. As we will see later in the story, Jonathan takes on a role similar to his armor-bearer's in his friendship with David.

Great teammates don't learn how to be great in isolation.

Great teammates don't learn how to be great in isolation. They pay attention to those around them who are doing it well. There's a level of humility involved in knowing that you can always learn something from someone else.

Gospel-Centered Teammates Are Skillful

> Then Jonathan climbed up on his hands and feet, and his armor-bearer after him. And they fell before Jonathan, and his armor-bearer killed them after him. And that first strike, which Jonathan and his armor-bearer made, killed about twenty men within as it were half a furrow's length in an acre of land (1 Sam. 14:13–14).

Jonathan was a warrior. It can be easy to forget that since the book of 1 Samuel spends so much time talking about how he supported and loved David. Jonathan was not a junior varsity athlete vying for a varsity spot. The kid was all-state. He was great at what he did. Why is this important? Because it's easy to assume that great teammates are just role players. We figure they have to be great teammates because that's the role they fill on the team. But that's far from the truth. Being a great teammate isn't limited to the armor-bearers and the ones who ride the bench. We are all called to be great teammates, no matter what our role is on the team.

Gospel-Centered Teammates Take Responsibility for Their Actions

> Then Saul said to Jonathan, "Tell me what you have done." And Jonathan told him, "I tasted a little honey with the tip of the staff that was in my hand. Here I am; I will die." And Saul said, "God do so to me and more also; you shall surely die, Jonathan" (1 Sam. 14:43–44).

After Jonathan's victory over the Philistines, King Saul forbid anyone within the army to eat anything until he avenged his enemies. Jonathan didn't get the memo and tasted some honey. He didn't blame anyone else, and he didn't try to justify his actions. He accepted the consequences, even if they seemed unfair. The rest of the men in the army intervened on his behalf, sparing his life.

Great teammates aren't perfect. They will make mistakes and do things they regret. They do not, however, hide under a rock when their misdeeds are exposed. They don't blame other teammates. They don't use social media as a passive-aggressive outlet. Even if the punishment seems unfair, they accept it and learn from it.

Gospel-Centered Teammates Fight against Entitlement

> As soon as he had finished speaking to Saul, the soul of Jonathan was knit to the soul of David, and Jonathan loved him as his own soul. And Saul took him that day and would not let him return to his father's house (1 Sam. 18:1–2).

This verse comes on the heels of David killing Goliath. By this point in the story, David is pegged as the next king of Israel. None of Saul's sons, including Jonathan, would succeed their father on the throne. The young shepherd who had killed lions and bears—and now Goliath—had the nation's attention. He had just moved into the starting lineup and taken Jonathan's spot. How did Jonathan respond? He loved David as he loved himself. He committed to being one in spirit with David. How would you respond?

The disease of entitlement runs rampant in the world of sports. I deserve this spot. I worked hard for my position. I am next in line when he or she graduates. I am better than they are. What they did was not that impressive.

It's so easy to become bitter at those who steal your spotlight or playing time. Great teammates seek to put others above themselves, especially in moments when it is most difficult to do so.

Gospel-Centered Teammates Don't Have a Hidden Agenda

> Then Jonathan made a covenant with David, because he loved him as his own soul. And Jonathan stripped himself of the robe that was on him and gave it to David, and his armor, and even his sword and his bow and his belt (1 Sam. 18:3–4).

Jonathan was all in on his friendship and loyalty to David. What we see in these verses is Jonathan giving up everything given to him and everything he worked for in order to help David advance. It's evident that Jonathan wasn't just trying to get on David's good side so he could leverage that position later. His words and his actions reflected his heart's desire.

Great teammates truly want what is best for others on the team. Their actions and words are not just a strategy to get back in the coach's good graces, but are an overflow of a desire to see others succeed, even if it comes at a significant cost.

Gospel-Centered Teammates Speak Well of Their Teammates Privately

> And Jonathan spoke well of David to Saul his father and said to him, "Let not the king sin against his servant David, because he has not sinned against you, and because his deeds have brought good to you" (1 Sam. 19:4).

As David continues to grow in popularity among the people, King Saul was increasingly jealous and wanted to kill David. This was Jonathan's chance to reclaim his spot. But he did not take the bait.

Great teammates don't lurk behind the scenes looking for an opportunity to capitalize on the misfortune of others. When necessary and appropriate, they advocate for their teammates behind closed doors. Anyone can champion a teammate in public. It takes a great teammate to do it when no one else is watching.

Gospel-Centered Teammates Let Their Teammates Know They Have Their Back

> Then Jonathan said to David, "Whatever you say, I will do for you" (1 Sam. 20:4).

When David was desperate, he came to Jonathan. He knew that Saul wanted him dead. Jonathan did not say "good luck" or "I will keep you in my prayers." He looked his friend in the eye and said he would do anything he asked him to do.

Great teammates don't put limits on what they will do for others. They are willing to be inconvenienced to help a teammate get out of a jam. This stands in stark contrast to the me-centered attitude of our sports culture. This willingness to help comes out of a growing awareness of the lengths to which Jesus went to serve and sacrifice for us. If sin didn't get in the way for him, surely we can't let sports get in the way for us.

Great teammates don't put limits on what they will do for others.

Gospel-Centered Teammates Enter into Their Teammates' Pain

> And Jonathan rose from the table in fierce anger and ate no food the second day of the month, for he was grieved for David, because his father had disgraced him (1 Sam. 20:34).

And as soon as the boy had gone, David rose from beside the stone heap and fell on his face to the ground and bowed three times. And they kissed one another and wept with one another, David weeping the most (1 Sam. 20:41).

Saul finally reached his tipping point. He expressed to Jonathan his disdain for him as a son and his intentions to kill David. In a moment when he had every right to isolate himself and recover from the personal attacks of his father, Jonathan chose to hurt with David. At that moment, he decided to enter into his friend's pain rather than his own.

Great teammates allow themselves to hurt and enter into the pain of others. If a teammate gets injured, they imagine what it must be like to be in that person's shoes. If a teammate loses or performs poorly, they encourage their teammate and try to lift his or her spirits. Great teammates don't try to fix the problem or minimize the pain. They use phrases like this: I'm really sorry. I can't imagine what you're going through. What do you need from me? I'm in your corner.

Gospel-Centered Teammates Celebrate Their Teammates' Success

The scriptures don't record many celebratory moments between David and Jonathan. It's pretty safe to assume, however, that when good things happened to David, Jonathan was joyfully celebrating with him.

Romans 12:15 implores believers to "rejoice with those who rejoice." Great teammates enter into the joy of others and celebrate with them. Sometimes a teammate's success will come at the cost of your own. If you can't muster up the energy in your heart to find happiness for your teammate, it becomes an opportunity for you to confess that to the Lord and repent. An inability to celebrate with others is a terrible, joy-robbing way to live. Great teammates embrace the call to "love your neighbor as yourself" (Matt. 19:19). Part of loving your neighbor—and your teammates—is being happy when good fortune comes their way.

What If I Honestly Don't Like Them?

Of course, all of this is easy when you like your teammates. What happens when you can't stand some of them? You can probably envision them in your head right now. The teammate who puts on a smile in front of you but gossips and spreads lies behind your back. The teammate who doesn't work nearly as hard as you do and yet has found favor with the coaching staff. The teammate who has a flair for the dramatic and seems addicted to the sympathy of others. The list goes on. The natural tendency is to avoid these kinds of teammates as much as possible. But what does it look like, practically, to glorify God in these hard situations? Christian athletes are called to a higher standard.

By looking at Jonathan's life, we see ten ways a gospel-centered teammate could act unselfishly toward others. But we need an additional approach in dealing with those teammates who consistently knock our hearts off the gospel-centered path. What are some things you can do to realign your heart in these instances?

Pray for Them.

In Matthew 5:44, Jesus says to his followers, "But I say to you, love your enemies and pray for those who persecute you." I would not classify a difficult teammate as an enemy, but the principle remains the same—pray for people who don't like you and for people you don't like. What should you pray? Ask God to move in their life, convict them about what they're doing wrong, and open the eyes of their hearts to see the grace that's freely offered. Then look for opportunities to share the gospel with them.

Pray for Yourself.
The possibility exists that God may want to do more in your heart in this situation than the teammate who is annoying you. Colossians 3:12–14 says, "Put on then, as God's chosen ones, holy and beloved, compassionate hearts, kindness, humility, meekness, and patience, bearing with one another and, if one has a complaint against another, forgiving each other; as the Lord has forgiven you, so you also must forgive. And above all these put on love, which binds everything together in perfect harmony." Pray that God would soften your heart toward this teammate, giving you patience, compassion, and the ability to see through this teammate's eyes.

Encourage Them.
By dying to yourself and showing kindness to someone who frustrates you, you will inevitably look different than most people. Again, that's the point. Christian athletes should be a light shining in a dark world. But more importantly, you will feel

Christian athletes should be a light shining in a dark world.

different because you choose to walk in obedience to God instead of allowing sin to take root in your heart. (If you need ideas for how to encourage a teammate, take a look at the previous chapter for some suggestions.)

Forgive Them.
Do you know who has every right to be frustrated with you? God. Do you know how many times a day your actions and thoughts are an affront to his holiness? If you are like me, often. Yet how does God deal with us? Romans 5:8 says, "But God shows his love for us in that while we were still sinners, Christ died for us." When did God demonstrate his love for us? Not after we cleaned up our act, but while we were in the act. We glorify God when we think and act in a way that pleases God

and draws attention to who he is. There are few greater ways to do this than to forgive someone who doesn't deserve it. Colossians 3:13 says that acting like a Christian means "bearing with one another and, if one has a complaint against another, forgiving each other; as the LORD has forgiven you, so you also must forgive."

Ask for Accountability.

Loving difficult teammates is challenging. As with any battle you are facing, trying to do it in isolation is only going to make it tougher. In his second letter to the Thessalonians, Paul shows his need for help when he said, "Finally, brothers, pray for us, that the word of the Lord may speed ahead and be honored, as happened among you, and that we may be delivered from wicked and evil men. For not all have faith" (2 Thess. 3:1–2).

Inviting another person into your present challenges greatly increases your chance of success. That's glorifying to God. What does it look like practically? Find another teammate, friend, coach, or parent, and say something like this:

> *I'm really struggling with this individual. You know how much they get under my skin. I want to make a better effort to love them like Jesus. Here is what I am going to try to do (fill in the blank). Would you make it a point to ask me how I am doing in this area once a week? Or better yet, would you remind me before practice starts to love them like Jesus?*

In a culture that celebrates the platforms that come with success, your greatest influence may be on the teammates with whom you rub shoulders every day. We all want to believe God has marvelous plans for us through success in our sport. What if he has you where you are so you can be a light to your teammates? Remember, it's ultimately about his glory, not your own.

CHAPTER 10

ON GRAY AREAS

An honorable defeat is better than a dishonorable victory.

—Millard Fillmore

For we aim at what is honorable not only in the Lord's sight but also in the sight of man.

—2 Corinthians 8:21

Brian Davis walked toward the green in the 2011 Verizon Heritage Golf Classic. He had just tied Jim Furyk on the 72nd hole to force a sudden-death playoff. But before he started to line up his putt, he called over the officials.

"I didn't feel anything, but I'm pretty sure that I saw that one reed move. I could be wrong because of the wind," Davis said.[1]

The officials looked at the replay and determined Davis' club did not hit the reed. They decided to take one more look, in super slow motion. Davis was right. His club hit a reed on his backswing.

The rule book identifies a reed like that one as a "loose impediment," and according to Rule 23 of the USGA's Rules of Golf, loose impediments can't be moved. The result was a two-stroke penalty. Nobody saw it, and Davis didn't feel it. But he thought he might have seen the reed move a little, so he self-reported it to the officials. Furyk went on to win the tournament.

Davis later estimated that the loss cost him close to $2 million. It was not just the tournament's prize money on the line but also an entrance into the Masters and endorsement bonuses. Davis said:

> But it's not so important that you cheat to achieve it. Golfers are expected to police themselves. It's in the gentleman's tradition of the game. It's what makes our sport unique. I'm a fan of the Arsenal Football Club and my father-in-law is Ray Clemence, who was a goalkeeper for Liverpool and England, so I know it's not the same in other sports. I'm not happy when a player goes down in the box after barely being brushed by a defender, but I know it's part of football's gamesmanship. It's not the same in golf. Even for anyone to *think* you're a cheater is horrible.[2]

Part of the Game?

Davis politely (like a golfer) refers to a soccer player acting like he took a bullet to gain an advantage on the field as "part of football's gamesmanship." But what about other sports?

Is it okay to steal signs in baseball or for pitchers to retaliate? What about holding a defensive linemen when the referee isn't looking? Is it okay to cut the wooded corner of the cross-country course if everyone ahead of you is cutting it? How about running up the score on a weak opponent? If you jump offsides or the ball hits you last before going out of bounds, is it just part of the game to point at the opposition as if they're to blame? All these scenarios fall under the category of gray areas within each sport's culture.

So, what's a gray area? The *Cambridge English Dictionary* defines a gray area as "a situation that is not clear or where the rules are not known."[3] In sports, the rules of the game are generally well-defined and well-known by the athletes. Usually, an athlete can't claim ignorance when it comes to rules. Sometimes, however, we run into a situation in sports that isn't quite so clear, like running up the score. There's no written rule against something like that, so it's a gray area to some extent. (Most would agree that while it may not go against the rules, it certainly violates the spirit of the game and is unsportsmanlike.) Another example of a gray area is when we see a basketball player flop or embellish some contact to try to get a favorable call. In the NBA, flopping is illegal, and everyone knows that. But some players still try to get away with it.

A gray area in sports can be described in one of two ways:

1. It's truly a situation where there are no clearly defined rules, like running up the score or tanking to get a better draft pick. It's not strictly prohibited but certainly frowned upon.

2. It's a situation in which the rules are most likely understood yet can be manipulated, exploited, or ignored to gain a tactical advantage. Each sport has some cultural norms that are understood by the players. Whether some tactic is blatantly against the rules or just part of the game, players sometimes seek to exploit these gray areas to achieve an advantage.

Each potential gray area has been debated extensively. I don't want to tackle this issue at the ground level, attempting to work my way through the positives and negatives on each side for every situation. Instead, I want to provide a big-picture view along with some questions that will help us respond to each gray area within our particular sport in a way that honors and glorifies God.

Passive Obedience vs. Active Obedience

Let's first talk about passive obedience to the rules versus active obedience. Passive obedience is when you play the game by the rules, but you don't think about it at the moment. You have been trained to play the game correctly, and in the heat of competition the overflow of your training enables you to compete within the set of rules without giving it a second thought. That's glorifying to God. The natural ability to play with a high level of integrity is the north star we want to look to as Christian athletes.

But what happens when playing by the rules doesn't come naturally? What do we do when we are faced with the option of valuing winning over integrity? That's where active obedience comes in. Active obedience in sports means you have to make a choice about what's right and what's wrong. It requires you to think and act.

Active obedience in sports means you have to make a choice about what's right and what's wrong.

How can we make the wise decision to play with integrity? Here are a few important questions to ask yourself when faced with a gray area in your sport.

Is what I am doing considered part of the game, or is it outright shady? Remember that verse, Romans 12:2, that talks about not being "conformed to this world"? Well, it applies here. If what you're doing is shady, stop doing it. I think there's a difference between shady, which is bordering on flat-out cheating, and how the game is actually played that needs to be taken seriously. But the line is extremely...gray.

Pitching at someone's head is shady. Giving another runner a sharp elbow so they go off the edge of the track or lane is shady. Purposefully cutting off a runner so he or she can't pass seems shady, but it's actually a regular tactical maneuver in track and field. Again, I don't want to get caught in the weeds by examining every potential situation.

Doing the right thing may mean forfeiting a tactical advantage, but you will look different from competitors who are willing to forfeit their integrity in a desperate attempt to win at all costs. The godly virtue of integrity applies to the sports arena just as much as anywhere else.

Is what I am doing against the written and unwritten rules?
If it is, stop doing it.

Am I aware that what I am doing is against the rules, or am I doing it by accident?
If you are aware, you need to repent and maybe even ask for forgiveness. In any case, stop doing it.

Has anyone ever gotten a foul, a penalty, or been disqualified for doing what I am doing?
Stop doing it.

Has anyone ever communicated to me that what I am doing is not right?
Stop doing it.

If I get caught doing this by a spectator or a slow-motion replay, will I feel convicted?
You have the Holy Spirit living in you. If you feel convicted, the probable cause is that he wants you to feel convicted. Stop doing it.

Do I sense in my heart a conviction to stop doing this?

Again, if you are a Christian, you have the Holy Spirit living within you. The conviction is coming from somewhere, most likely him. Stop doing it.

The Bible says God created us in his image. The implications of this reality are far-reaching. One implication is that we are to image God by acting like him.

Genesis 1:2 gives us a glimpse of how God works: "The earth was without form and void, and darkness was over the face of the deep. And the Spirit of God was hovering over the face of the waters." Verse 3 says, "And God said, 'Let there be light,' and there was light." God stared into the chaos and created order. He's still doing that today.

What does that look like in sports? Simply put, we follow the rules of the game. We compete by the rules all the time because they express what is orderly, fair, and just. As an image-bearer of the most high God, are you acting like him by bringing order, or are you contributing to the chaos? When we image his character, we glorify who he is. Do you remember the definition of giving glory to God? It's thinking and acting in a way that pleases God and draws attention to who he is. When we choose to operate with integrity in every way possible, we image our creator.

As an image-bearer of the most high God, are you acting like him by bringing order, or are you contributing to the chaos?

With respect to gray areas in sports, it means we place a higher premium on being obedient to God than being successful at the expense of our integrity. How we act reveals our priorities. It almost sounds too simple. Play your sport within the set of rules prescribed, and you will bring glory to

God. When faced with an opportunity to bend the rules, you have two options:

1. Bend the rules to bring glory to yourself.
2. Obey the rules to bring glory to God.

The way a Christian athlete responds to gray areas can set him or her apart from the rest of the world. It's one of the reasons being obedient to God in all circumstances within our sport can be so impactful. When we act in countercultural ways, people take notice. Our influence often grows as a result of our obedience.

Two Words of Caution

In an article on sportsmanship, Dr. Ed Uszynski wrote:

> Doing the right thing doesn't mean you'll come out on top of the scoreboard. We can't make a deal with God or demand a pact whose contractual obligations read something like "If I do the right thing, you (God) will make sure I win the game." What you can be assured of when you live surrendered to God's standards is His favor extended toward you in any number of other ways: peace in the midst of trials, guilt-free living, wisdom to say the right thing, grace for each moment of the day, the contentment that comes from being in his will. You may win games too, but wins and losses in the Kingdom of God look far different than they do on the sports page. God evaluates winners and losers according to a completely different scoring system. His desires are not displayed through us by tallying numbers on a board, but in choosing righteousness, justice, and godly character when faced with opportunities to do so.[4]

Of course, doing the right thing can be difficult because we're often tempted to protect our own kingdom instead of building his. Nevertheless, integrity never goes out of style in God's economy, and he will bless our obedience in one way or another.

Another caution for athletes who take a hard line on gray areas is the propensity to become prideful. This can take a couple different forms. First, we can compare ourselves to other athletes, teammates, or competitors who are not striving for the same level of integrity that we are. This comparison game inevitably leads to thinking we are better than the person next to us. You may be choosing a better path, but believing you are more righteous than someone else is dangerous. It's also sinful. The joy received from playing the game with the highest possible level of integrity ought to come from knowing you are glorifying your Father, not from feeling like you are better than everyone else.

The second form our pride can take is anger—anger directed at those who do not choose to play with the same high level of integrity. If somebody takes a shortcut, bends the rules, or cheats in some way, it is okay to be frustrated. Being angry is the right response to injustice. God has hardwired us to reflect his image, and when an injustice occurs, a frustrated response is a good and right response. That being said, the bad anger I'm referring to asks, "If I can play by the rules, why can't they?" It says, "Look, I'm doing it right. They should be able to do it right too." That's pride. There's a big difference between being frustrated by injustice and feeling frustrated because others can't measure up to your standards. Your frustration needs to be grounded in "that's wrong" and not "be like me."

So how should a Christian athlete approach gray areas within their sport? With the highest possible standard of integrity. Doing so glorifies God. And your integrity, empowered by God's grace in your life, may give you opportunities to explain why you choose to play the way you do despite competing in a culture that values winning above everything else.

CHAPTER 11

ON RETIREMENT

[One] key to a meaningful transition is to retire to
something and not from something.

—Bob Russell

D eath. Taxes. Athletes retiring.
I know you don't want to read this chapter. The title
alone reminds you of the truth that one day the sport
you play will become the sport you used to play. I don't know
how it will end for you. It could be a career-ending injury.
Maybe time will finally catch up with you and force you to
call it quits, or maybe a diminishing skill level will prevent
you from advancing to your next career goal. Whether you
choose to hang up the cleats or it is somehow chosen for you,
one day you will no longer be a competitive athlete. And that
will probably be difficult to come to terms with.

Many of us struggle with the finality of our athletic career coming to a close. So we continue to chase after ways to keep it alive, often at lower levels of competition. Is there still the desire to make it to the pinnacle of success in our sport? There could be. But the more likely reality is that we don't want to stop competing—period. The reality is that retirement is inevitable for every athlete. We all know the day is approaching, but it's hard to anticipate and process the feelings that come with competing in a sport coming to an end. Prim Siripipat, a former collegiate tennis player, once said, "As tough as college was, no one warned me about an even greater challenge ahead: saying goodbye to the sport I love and making that transition into the 'real world.' The mental and emotional toll of this transition was a shock to my system."[1]

But what Siripipat said could probably be attributed to anyone who has ever played competitive sports.

Dr. Henry Cloud points out in his book *How People Grow* that "One of the most important processes in life is grief. God has designed grief to help us get over things."[2]

And make no mistake about it, moving on from your athletic career can be a grieving process. If done correctly, however, you will move through it in a way that honors God.

The purpose of this chapter is to help us glorify God through retirement. Part of that process involves practical advice on outward actions we would be wise to follow. But we first need to understand what is going on inside our hearts. Why is retirement so difficult for athletes?

A 2007 study found that "the transition is often found to be difficult because of the sudden cessation of intense demands of elite athletic performance, compounded by the sudden loss of the athlete's intense devotion to professional athletic competition and its attendant rewards."[3]

What does all that mean? Understanding the process can help us transition from our sport to whatever God has in store for us next.

What Are We Leaving Behind?

The Hype (Rewards)

Boxing legend Sugar Ray Leonard famously said, "Nothing could satisfy me outside the ring. There is nothing in life that can compare to becoming a world champion, having your hand raised in that moment of glory, with thousands, millions of people cheering you on."[4] While many of you will not be able to resonate with the feeling that comes from being a world champion and having millions of fans cheer you on, all athletes are in a unique position in culture to claim that at least some people have cheered for them. It's one of the rewards we desire most: the approval of others. You have no doubt experienced the hype leading up to a big competition and subsequently the hype of the contest itself. Even if you were not the center of attention, you were still part of the action. You played a role in the hype. And the hype is addictive.

For many of you, your new normal will not include crowds of people affirming you when you do your job well. The rewards for a job well done will look different. If you get an A on a test, maybe your family will pat you on the back. If you do well in your job, your affirmation may take the form of a bigger paycheck, but it definitely won't include everyone carrying you on their shoulders out of the office. The question that will—and should—haunt you in your next stage of life is this: For whom am I ultimately doing this?

Colossians 3:17 says, "And whatever you do, in word or deed, do everything in the name of the Lord Jesus, giving thanks to God the Father through him." Our motivation, whether in sports, school, work, or relationships should be to serve Jesus, not ourselves. Adjusting to life after the hype will be challenging, but it may be the very adjustment that helps you realign your motivation for the rest of your life.

The Competition (Elite Athletic Performance)

Athletes are in a unique position to experience frequent highs and lows. Who else can ride the roller coaster of emotions on such a regular basis where it almost becomes normal? Maybe day traders. Maybe parents. For some, the drama that comes with sports will not be missed. But for others, the addictive rush is hard to give up. Dr. Ed Uszynski writes:

> If you're an athlete, no rush compares to being physically challenged by another human who spends their days training to beat you—then either discovering you are equal to the challenge or having the areas you need to improve on exposed, thereby shaping the next days' workout. The athletic psyche stalks challenge, seeks goals that push beyond barriers posed by normal life. Craving this bar-raising lifestyle can become almost addictive—and like other addictions, the grip happens without their knowledge or consent and is hard to get "fixed." After decades of playing with elite-level players, kicking around at the local YMCA and retiring to backyard pick-up ball—while easily romanticized—is depressing, and every athlete who sees that future runs from it for as long as possible.[5]

The ups and downs set a standard that could make the next stage of your life feel comparatively dull.

The Rhythms (Sudden Cessation of Intense Demands)

Dr. Uszynski goes on to explain the challenge:

> There is a certain comfort that accompanies the boundaries to an athletic lifestyle. This can be replaced but it's not easy to find or come up with

on one's own. Retirement represents the death of an entire scheduling, relational, and subcultural lifestyle.[6]

At first, you will love the freedom that comes with being done with your sport. You get to sleep past 7:00 a.m. You get to eat more freely. You get to choose when and where you want to work out—or if you want to work out at all. But you will eventually miss the structure and the accountability within that structure. You will miss the rhythms of being a competitive athlete.

One might imagine that loosening the knot around the rigid structure would feel liberating, but often that is not the case. Athletes usually enjoy the free schedule at the beginning before ending up feeling lost without having to do things related to their sport—and for good reason. When your entire life is categorized by practices, workouts, nutrition guidelines, rest and recovery phases, and the orders of coaches and trainers, you are at high risk of becoming dependent on those structured systems in order to thrive.

Matt Perman, author of *What's Best Next*, helps us understand why we thrive under structure. "Systems trump intentions. You can have great intentions, but if your life is set up in a way that is not in alignment with them, you will be frustrated. The structure of your life will win out every time."[7]

You will be tempted to binge-watch Netflix and sleep until it's time to eat lunch. Don't. Your athletic career may be over, but God's calling on your life to be productive with your day still demands a response.

Did you catch that last sentence? Structure matters. You will be tempted to binge-watch Netflix and sleep until it's time to eat lunch. Don't. Your athletic career may be over, but God's calling on your life to be productive with your day still demands a response.

Ephesians 5:15–16 says, "Look carefully then how you walk, not as unwise but as wise, making the best use of the time, because the days are evil." The intense demands and structure of your sport may be done, but don't use that as an excuse to become lazy. Glorify God by moving your disciplined structure of living into a new passion or hobby that serves others and makes much of Jesus.

The Sense of Purpose (Intense Devotion)

Our purpose will always flow from our identity. How we view ourselves determines what we do—and being an athlete is usually a huge part of a person's self-concept. Even in this book, I have addressed you as an athlete. The implications of this can be damning. The following thoughts from Dr. Monica Frank should resonate:

> It is critical to recognize that the athlete's self-identity is typically inseparable from their role as an athlete. Often for many years the major focus in their life is on developing as an athlete and succeeding in their chosen sport. When the sports career ends, it leaves a major hole in the athlete's life. Whether the career ended as planned or suddenly, the athlete experiences a significant loss that can be as devastating as losing a loved one. The end of the career doesn't mean just not engaging in the sport anymore. It also changes the athlete's role: he or she is no longer an "athlete."[8]

If God graciously allows you to experience his love and grace through sports, while glorifying him through your athletic career, that's awesome. But whether you identify as an athlete, father, mother, friend, accountant, janitor, husband, or wife, your ultimate purpose never changes. Christian, you were placed on this earth to glorify God through loving him and serving others. Your purpose does not change—only the vehicle that drives you there.

Your permanent purpose is to glorifyGod by loving God and loving others. You used to spend much of your time and energy attempting to do this through your sport. Now that sports are in the rearview mirror, you need a new vehicle to drive you toward this purpose.

What's Next?

Preparation will always make transitions easier. Dr. Henry Cloud and Dr. John Townsend point out, "We must have something good in hand to be able to let go of something bad. It is a little like being a trapeze artist: You can only let go of one trapeze if another is in view."[9]

The easiest way to move on from sports is to replace the role that sports played with something else. Here is the reality. When your sport ends, you will have space in your life that did not exist before. You will have time. And that time needs to be stewarded well. The remainder of this chapter could be filled with jab after jab about ideas and strategies to cope with the transition and move forward. But I want to give you a right hook. I want to give you one big, God-glorifying way to transition out of your athletic career wisely.

Ready? I want to challenge you to get involved in the local church.

I know some of you may cringe at that statement. Some of you may have had a bad experience with a church or may have avoided going or getting involved for various other reasons. Let me say this as gently as I can: get over it. The church is God's primary vehicle to reach the world.

The church is God's primary vehicle to reach the world.

Francis Chan doesn't mince words when talking about the importance of the church: "We can't claim to follow Jesus if we neglect the church He created, the church He died for, the church He entrusted His mission to....The church is God's strategy for reaching our world."[10]

You no longer have the excuse of competing and traveling on the weekends. You no longer can leverage your coach's early Sunday morning workouts as a way out. For some of you, these may have been the excuses you needed to get you out of being more involved in a church. For others, they were legitimate and to some extent unavoidable for a season of life. To some degree, every athlete's church involvement is negatively affected by the demands of his or her sport.

The church is the primary way God has chosen to reach the world with his love. If that's not motivation enough to get involved, there is another factor that may capture your attention. Some of the same things you came to love and enjoy through sports can be experienced at an even deeper level through involvement with the local church. The dangling carrot of contentment you so desperately sought through sports can be obtained through the local church. Let me explain by working back through some of the benefits of sports that you will be leaving behind.

The Hype (Rewards)

Can anything compare with achieving an athletic goal and having teammates, coaches, and fans affirm the accomplishment? Absolutely. If you have ever played a role in helping someone grow in their faith and seeing God transform their life, you know firsthand that no athletic performance will ever compare. Transformation will always win out over trophies.

As God's primary strategy to reach a lost world, the church stands on the front lines. By linking arms with the church, you are putting yourself in prime position to see God transform the lives of men and women in your community, country, and the world. If you are looking to set high goals and willing to rely on God and trust him to come through for you, you will not find many better options than getting involved with the local church.

The Competition (Elite Athletic Performance)
We love to associate athletic talent as a gift from God. It certainly is, but when the Bible speaks of gifts from the Lord, it is not talking about genetic dispositions but spiritual additions. For too long, you have been led to believe that the gifts God has given you are primarily your athletic skills. It is time to learn that God has given you a different set of gifts—a gift to be stewarded not for your own glory or the benefit of screaming fans, but for the good of God's people. Romans 12:6–8 encourages us to use our spiritual gifts for the benefit of others.

> Having gifts that differ according to the grace given to us, let us use them: if prophecy, in proportion to our faith; if service, in our serving; the one who teaches, in his teaching; the one who exhorts, in his exhortation; the one who contributes, in generosity; the one who leads, with zeal; the one who does acts of mercy, with cheerfulness.

Each of us, if we have been reconciled to God through belief in the gospel, has been given spiritual gifts by the Holy Spirit for the benefit of his people. One of the best settings to learn what spiritual gifts you have is within the context of a local church where you can walk in community with other Christ-followers and grow together.

The Rhythms (Sudden Cessation of Intense Demands)

Your life—and schedule—used to be centered around the demands of your sport. Check out what 1 Timothy 4:8 says: "For while bodily training is of some value, godliness is of value in every way, as it holds promise for the present life and also for the life to come." Your structured way of living around sports produced some value. What if your new structure involved significant involvement and blocks of time given to the church? This verse clearly shows that a pursuit of godliness has both present value and eternal value. The church provides a rhythmic structure to help you in this area. Commit to attending church weekly and finding a place to serve there. Get plugged into a weekly small group. Ask where the church has a need and be willing to help.

The Sense of Purpose (Intense Devotion)

If you are a Christian, the calling on your life will continue to flow from the Great Commission found in Matthew 28:19–20. In these verses, Jesus instructs *all* his followers to "Go therefore and make disciples of all nations, baptizing them in the name of the Father and of the Son and of the Holy Spirit, teaching them to observe all that I have commanded you. And behold, I am with you always, to the end of the age."

John Piper boldly lays out our three options in response to this: "There are three possibilities with the Great Commission. You can go. You can send. Or you can be disobedient. Ignoring the cause is not a Christian option."[11]

You can help fulfill the Great Commission through the avenue of sports. The purpose of the church is to love God and love your neighbor while working to see the Great Commission fulfilled. The church's mission focuses on this goal. Against the backdrop of eternity, knowing God and doing his will, including sharing the good news with others, easily trumps any other goal you could strive for. If you are feeling lost and confused in the midst of your retirement, why not join the greatest mission in the history of the world? The church is waiting for you.

J. Campbell White said it well:

> Most men are not satisfied with the permanent output of their lives. Nothing can wholly satisfy the life of Christ within his followers except the adoption of Christ's purpose toward the world he came to redeem. Fame, pleasure, and riches are but husks and ashes in contrast with the boundless and abiding joy of working with God for the fulfillment of his eternal plans. The men who are putting everything into Christ's undertaking are getting out of life its sweetest and most priceless rewards.[12]

Athlete—I mean, Christian—mourn the loss of your sport. But mourn quickly. Lift your head and direct your time, talents, and energy into church involvement, and be part of the greatest mission this world has ever known.

CHAPTER 12

ON COACHES

*This is the secret of being content: to learn and accept
that we live daily by God's unmerited favor given
through Christ and that we can respond to any and
every situation by His divine enablement through the
Holy Spirit.*

—Jerry Bridges

The blog wasn't particularly long, coming in at just under 650 words. While it wasn't written poorly, it wasn't written by someone who was overly concerned about sentence flow or grammar either. This was a flat-out rant. And it struck a nerve. Apparently, when you strike a nerve, the form of the blow isn't all that important.

On August 15, 2016, Madison Trout, a college basketball player, hit *publish* on a blog post that would resonate with hundreds of thousands of athletes across the country. It was called "The Coach That Killed My Passion," and the subtitle was "An open letter to the coach that made me hate a sport I once loved." The blog spread virally through social media channels, with each additional like and share serving as affirmation from other individuals who have felt similar disdain for how their coaches treated them. The post shed light on an all too familiar narrative—a coaching style that neglects encouragement and motivates from fear. Trout wanted to say this to the coach: "Making me feel bad about myself doesn't make me want to play and work hard for you, whether in the classroom or on the court."[1]

This issue is personal for me as well. My first cross country practice started with me and all the other newbies on top of a picnic table. The rest of the team circled around us. The coach then walked up to each of us and tugged our shorts down, revealing to everyone whether we were wearing boxers or briefs. It was humiliating.

Four years later, I found myself in the ACC championship cross country race. With two miles to go, I heard my coach yell out to me, "Brian, you're killing us!" To his credit, I *was* killing our team. Simply pointing out the reality, however, was not motivating. I have to wonder how I would have finished if he had yelled something to encourage me and give me hope.

If a coach's ultimate goal is to achieve an optimal level of play, we need to admit that sometimes fear is an effective motivator. It is unwise and ineffective in the long term, at least, to reinforce an athlete's fear of failure with more fear tactics. Instead, constructive and encouraging coaching is a much better way to bring about the results coaches want. Sometimes, the most effective parenting strategy is to threaten to take away something your child loves if he or she doesn't change an unhealthy behavior. If this becomes a habitual strategy, however, I am no longer acting like a parent; I begin to resemble a tyrant.

There is a time and a place when fear is an appropriate means of motivating, but what my experience has taught me is that most of the time, fear gets wielded as a weapon, not as an instrument of change. Athlete, there are four reasons why I think some coaches drift toward motivating by fear and, in the process, make your life miserable. As you will learn shortly, none of those reasons give you a license to fight back.

Fear of Failure

One of the most challenging realities for coaches is the fact that their paychecks depend on the performances of the athletes they coach. For the vast majority of coaches, that means their ability to pay the mortgage and put food on the table rests in the hands and feet of the young men and women they coach. If they don't win early and often, they could be out and replaced.

Insecurity

Coaching is a dangerous profession for an individual to enter into if they struggle with insecurity. Why? People who are insecure are constantly looking for validation from others. A quick Google search of specific coaches shows you what they are ultimately measured by—the number of wins and losses they have accrued over the years. For someone who struggles with insecurity, the win-loss record becomes an extension of their identity. So when the team struggles or an individual athlete underperforms, they have a tendency to lash out. One of the quickest ways to feel better about themselves is to make someone else feel small.

Immaturity

I'm concerned that using fear reflects the sad reality that many coaches lack the ability to control their emotions in the heat of the moment. This is unfortunate. Athletes don't get a free pass for being out of control on the field. Likewise, coaches should not get a free pass for uncontrolled outbursts under the guise of motivation.

I have been involved in sports at some level for the past 25 years. One thing I have noticed is most coaches who motivate their athletes by fear are not trying to motivate at all; they are unloading their own anger issues at the easiest target. I get this, even as a parent. When my kid spills milk on the carpet, my gut reaction is to yell, "If you do that again, you will never be given milk again!" Is that motivating by fear? Sure. At my core, however, I'm just trying to feel better and regain a sense of control by unleashing my anger on the easiest target. My job at that moment is to be the adult, rise above my frustration, and assess the best course of action to take for the betterment of my child.

Power

While insecurity and immaturity use fear reactively, the desire to leverage power over a vulnerable athlete is often a proactive tactic. Every coach in authority over a player—especially in non-professional environments—understands intuitively that he or she has power over that player. The coach controls whether you are on the team at all as well as your playing time and, to some extent, your overall experience. Often, players feel powerless to fight back when they are verbally, emotionally, or even physically abused by a coach.

A Higher Standard

This book is not for coaches. It is written to you, the athlete—specifically, the Christian athlete. And Christian athletes—as you should know by now—are called by God to a higher standard. Regardless of whether your coach motivates through fear, insecurity, immaturity, or power, your response should remain consistent with how the Bible instructs us to act when we're under someone else's authority. Philippians 2:14–15 is crystal clear: "Do all things without grumbling or disputing, that you may be blameless and innocent, children of God without blemish in the midst of a crooked and twisted generation, among whom you shine as lights in the world."

Regardless of whether your coach motivates through fear, insecurity, immaturity, or power, your response should remain consistent with how the Bible instructs us to act when we're under someone else's authority.

Your coach may be a jerk who treats you unfairly. Your coach may purposely try to make your life miserable because he or she doesn't like you. But guess what? Jesus was in a similar situation. He was falsely accused and betrayed. He did not fight back. He did not argue. He did not complain.

He did not rant on his blog about his unfair predicament or lash out on social media. He stayed faithful and obedient to God in the midst of a horrifically unfair situation. We would do well to follow his lead.

It's our job as God's lights in this dark world to submit to authority, stay positive, and display the life and love of Jesus in harsh and unfair situations. Complaining and demanding that we get what we think we deserve shows an immature understanding of how we ought to respond to the authority over us.

Athlete, save yourself the mental energy of figuring out all the reasons your coach is wrong and you are right. Your biblical mandate in these instances is to faithfully submit to your coach, even if his or her methods are less than ideal. The evidence in your case may very well prove that your coach is acting like a jerk, but it is a dangerous leap to believe God is more concerned with your coach's actions than with yours.

We need a faith-filled, submissive response to a coach who consistently insists upon a coaching method that brings frustration. What does it look like to glorify God by how we respond, inwardly and outwardly, to our coaches?

Inward Realignments

I understand that we all want practical ways to glorify God. But if we have a bitter and frustrated heart, we are missing out on fully glorifying God and robbing ourselves of joy in the process. Two realignments need to take place inside of us, which will hopefully lead to some practical outward actions.

Shift Expectations

I heard this life-changing truth a few years ago, and it has helped me in every category of my life. *Every disappointment in life is a result of unmet expectations.* This does not mean always lowering expectations—though in some instances that can be beneficial—but it does mean that your expectations need to be realistic. Your coach's job is to win, and the decisions he or she makes along the way will be toward that end.

At the end of the day, your performance determines your coach's future. Your coach's job is not to be your friend, your biggest cheerleader, or your counselor. You need to get rid of those expectations. You will free yourself up from a lot of inevitable disappointment if you release these good but unrealistic expectations about your coach. Those needs for a friend, a cheerleader, or a counselor can and should be filled by your friends, your parents, and your teammates—not your coach.

Shift Perspective

The other internal change that needs to happen is to shift the object of our obedience from our coach to the Lord. Ephesians 6:7–8 encourages workers (and athletes) to "[render] service with a good will as to the Lord and not to man, knowing that whatever good anyone does, this he will receive back from the Lord, whether he is a bondservant or is free." You can see here that Paul is encouraging his readers to serve as if God is the one we are serving.

We see a similar exhortation in Colossians 3:22–24: "Bondservants, obey in everything those who are your earthly masters, not by way of eye-service, as people-pleasers, but with sincerity of heart, fearing the Lord. Whatever you do, work heartily, as for the Lord and not for men, knowing that from the

Lord you will receive the inheritance as your reward. You are serving the Lord Christ."

How does Paul encourage these Christian bondservants of his time? He pleads with them to look past their earthly authorities to their heavenly authority. He asks them to work "as for the Lord" because they are really "serving the Lord Christ."

As you think ahead to practices and competitions, seek to be obedient to the Lord through humble submission to your coach. Life was probably a lot tougher for first-century Christian bondservants than it is for you as an athlete under the authority of a coach, yet the call to submission remains the same. Athlete, honor the Lord by honoring your coach, even if the coach is undeserving—*especially* if the coach is undeserving.

As you wrestle with realigning your expectations and perspective in this area, what are some practical action steps you can begin to incorporate into your life to glorify God through the way you interact with your coach?

Work Hard

Colossians 3:23–24 also gives us advice to work hard: "Whatever you do, work heartily, as for the Lord and not for men, knowing that from the Lord you will receive the inheritance as your reward. You are serving the Lord Christ."

Athlete, if your coach has negative things to say about you, let it be about your level of skill, not about your work ethic or attitude.

You glorify God when you work hard and when your motivation for doing so is because you are seeking to please the Lord. Athlete, if your coach has negative things to say about you, let it be about your level of skill, not about your work ethic or attitude.

Be a Learner

Proverbs 10:17 says, "Whoever heeds instruction is on the path to life, but he who rejects reproof leads others astray." Ask questions. Learn how you can get better at what you are already good at. One of the markers of humility is taking on the posture of a learner. When you show the desire to be a continual learner, you honor your coach as the teacher—and you glorify God.

When You Screw Up, Own It

You will perform poorly at times, and when you do, there's a chance your coach will let you have it verbally. This is not the time to lash back with excuses, even if they are justifiable.

Having a bad practice or a miserable competition is not a sin that you need to confess. But the expectation placed on you by your coach demands a certain level of excellence. When your level of play does not match that expectation, own it. Don't talk back. Don't sulk or pout. Tell your coach you know you need to—and can—do better next time.

Honor Your Coaches When They Are Not Present

Proverbs 18:8 warns, "The words of a whisperer are like delicious morsels; they go down into the inner parts of the body." In his book *Resisting Gossip*, Matthew Mitchell offers us a helpful definition surrounding the word *gossip*: "Sinful gossip is bearing bad news behind someone's back out of a bad heart."[2] Listen, I know how strong the temptation is to unload on a coach behind his or her back. I was often guilty of this. It's the easy way out. It's the natural way people operate. However, Christian athletes, as we've been saying, are called to stand out from the crowd, to look different. I wish I would have heeded the words of Ephesians 4:29: "Let no corrupting talk come out of your mouths, but only such as is good for building up, as fits the occasion, that it may give grace to those who hear."

Be Thankful

First Thessalonians 5:18 says, "Give thanks in all circumstances; for this is the will of God in Christ Jesus for you." Be a thankful person and a thankful athlete. If your coach is going to be annoyed with you, let it be because you are able to have a positive attitude in seemingly dire circumstances. Be known as hope-filled, humble, and thankful. Don't allow yourself to become lumped in with the complainers. Vocally express thanks to your coach for a great workout, even if he or she spent the whole time yelling at you.

Pray for Your Coach

In Matthew 5:44, Jesus commanded: "Love your enemies and pray for those who persecute you." It may seem like a stretch to classify a bad coach as an enemy. It's probably an even greater stretch to associate the word *persecution* with mistreatment as an athlete. Regardless, the principle of praying for those whom you find it difficult to like remains in effect. So pray for your coach's joy. Pray that you would find favor in your coach's eyes. Pray for his or her salvation. Pray for forgiveness for any sinful attitudes and actions related to your coach.

Let's go back to Madison Trout's story about the coach that stole her passion for her sport. Here's what she said in her open letter:

> When a passion dies, it is quite possibly the most heartbreaking thing ever. A desire you once had to play every second of the day is gone; it turns into dreading every practice and game. It turns into leaving every game with earphones in so other parents don't talk to you about it. It meant dreading school the next day due to everyone talking about the previous game.[3]

Trout allowed her coach to steal the keys to the joy of her sport. Don't make the same mistake. Fight for your joy by honoring your coach in every circumstance. In doing so, you will glorify your Father in heaven.

CHAPTER 13

ON MISSION

I've been put here for a specific purpose: to be a witness
and to share my testimony as I go through it.

—Stephen Curry

Acts 17:26 says, "And he made from one man every nation of mankind to live on all the face of the earth, having determined allotted periods and the boundaries of their dwelling place." God marked out our appointed times in history. God has a purpose for his people, and we see that in the time and location of their placement. Athlete, it is no mistake that God has given you the abilities you possess. It is also no mistake that God has placed you where you are. Why has he placed you there? To be a minister of reconciliation. Second Corinthians 5:18 says he "gave us the ministry of reconciliation."

Us. You. Me. This is not a purpose or ministry given only to "professional" Christians but to all professing Christians. And professing Christians must know what to profess.

Where Do We Start?

I had just finished meeting with Warren when he stood up and exclaimed, "I am a dangerous man now!" Warren is a big guy—six feet two inches tall and 300 pounds of muscle. He plays football—as if there were any other sport he could play at that size. As a defensive tackle, his job is to push other 300-pound men out of the way and try to tackle whoever has the football in front of him. In an ideal world, he would crush the opposing player hard enough to dislodge the football. Yes, Warren is a very dangerous man.

But we were not talking about football. Warren had just been trained how to communicate what he believed in four simple steps. It was he gospel: (1) God loves you; (2) your sin separates you from him; (3) Jesus paid the price for a restored relationship; and (4) there is a decision to make. Upon learning this, something clicked inside of him. For the first time, he realized he had been equipped to fight battles, not on an earthly playing field, but on an eternal one. Yes, Warren had just become really dangerous.

God gave you an athletic gift, and you are using it in a culture that worships sports heroes. Whether you like it or not, you are a difference-maker. How are you stewarding that reality? As athletes, we bring glory to God when we speak well of him in public (Psalm 40:16). We should absolutely live a lifestyle on and off the field that honors God. But we must also use words. When my son publically tells his friends he has the best dad ever, it is a higher honor to me than when he merely tells me in the privacy of our house.

God has given you a gift, a relationship with him, and a mouth to declare his goodness to a world that desperately needs it. We bring glory to him when we leverage this reality.

The purpose of this book has been to help you learn how to glorify God in all the circumstances your sport provides. If you put even some of these ideas into practice, people will notice. And when they notice, they will become curious. So you'd better be prepared. What if somebody came up to you and said, "You seem different than other people, why is that?" How would you respond? First Peter 3:15 says we should always be prepared to answer a question like that. Here are two simple ways to be properly prepared to provide a reply:

1. Know God's story.

Simply put, know the gospel. Warren became dangerous because he learned how to communicate with someone else what he already knew to be true.

2. Know your story.

Aside from knowing the gospel, which is "the power of God" (Romans 1:16), you need to learn your own story of how you came into a relationship with God. Your story helps explain why you are different.

Athlete, if you claim to be a Christian and yet are unable to articulate either of these at some level, you are not very dangerous to the enemy. You are entering a war carrying a squirt gun and water balloons. To be an effective spiritual leader on your team, you need to learn how to articulate the gospel and how to put your story into words. Be able to do those two things and you are well on your way to becoming dangerous. The website for Athletes in Action has a resource section designed to help athletes become competent in communicating both the gospel and their testimony. If this is

> *To be an effective spiritual leader on your team, you need to learn how to articulate the gospel and how to put your story into words.*

an area where you need training, please check it out at https://athletesinaction.org/resources/equipped.

What's Next?

You have been strategically placed on your team to impact the culture of your team. To borrow a biblical metaphor, you are a light in a dark place. In Matthew 5:16, Jesus shares this with his followers: "In the same way, let your light shine before others, so that they may see your good works and give glory to your Father who is in heaven." The ultimate goal of being a light on your team is not for your teammates to look up to you, but to look through you and glorify God. How can you move in this direction? Let's talk strategy for a minute.

You will not change the current culture on your team by trying to change it. What I mean by that is that you will not alter the culture of your team by telling them to change the music in the weight room or imploring them to stop swearing in the locker room. Nor will you change the culture by telling teammates to stop partying or stop putting harmful substances into their bodies. The you-need-to-stop-that strategy has proved to be ineffective. It makes you look arrogant for seemingly placing yourself above them and judging them, and it furthers the distance between them and God's best for their lives.

The best way to change the culture on your team is to create a new culture. Notice that there's a difference between trying to change the old or existing culture and creating an entirely new culture. The strategy shift is quite simple. Instead of serving as the morality police on your team, create new opportunities for them to think and act differently. Instead of walking into the darkness and saying, "Get out of here," shine a light on a better option. At some point, most everyone reaches a valley so low that they become starved for something that will satisfy. And many will be willing to try anything—even Jesus—at that point. So your role is to be ready to offer them something different when they are ready.

How do you go about creating a new culture? Here are a few ideas:

- Lead a prayer time before or after the game.
- Invite an injured friend over for dinner. Better yet, bring the dinner to your friend.
- Take every freshman out for coffee and ask them how their year is going and what you can do to help.
- Start a Bible study or find someone to start it for your team.
- Find a campus ministry, start attending their meetings, and invite teammates to go with you.

The 1989 classic movie *Field of Dreams* is about a farmer in Iowa who really loves baseball. One day, while out in his field, he hears a voice proclaim, "If you build it, he will come." He eventually discerns that what he needs to build is a baseball field in the middle of his cornfield. People think he is crazy because nobody has ever done that before. It was not a regular part of the farming culture to turn a field of crops into a baseball field.

Building a new culture doesn't guarantee that people will come. That's not your job anyway. God will always be the one who moves in people's hearts, spurring them to take action. Your responsibility and the way you will glorify God is to faithfully work at providing a space for them to move to when God gives them that nudge.

A team Bible study could be one of the most effective ways to create a new culture on your team.

A Few Thoughts on Bible Studies

There is a direct correlation between an individual's stagnant, immature faith and the lack of time they devote to reading the Bible. A team Bible study could be one of the most effective ways to create a new culture on your team. But leading one of these groups can be scary and intimidating. I want to help demystify the team Bible study by giving you a few simple tracks to run down.

1. **Let people know about it.** Put the day, time, and location on the board in the locker room. Send out an email to the team. Make sure everyone knows it exists. Then individually invite your teammates. Asking each one personally creates a greater likelihood that they will come. It may feel a little awkward, especially if they decline your invitation, but get over it. Eternity is at stake.

2. **Be consistent.** Have your study on the same day, at the same time, and at the same location every week. If you are constantly changing times and places, it will confuse your teammates. Confusion is a barrier for them showing up. Make it as easy as possible by keeping the schedule the same.

3. **Show up and stay there.** If your Bible study is on Monday nights from 7:00 to 8:00 p.m., get there at 6:50 and stay there until 8:00, even if you are the only one who shows up.

4. **All you need is one other person.** If one teammate shows up, start the Bible study with that person. Don't sulk and make comments like, "Well, I guess we're the only ones," or "I wish more people would have come." Be excited for the person who came. God has a plan for that person— and for you.

5. **Read the Bible.** Don't overcomplicate a Bible study. Study the Bible. Work your way through one of the Gospels. Do a chapter each week. Read the chapter out loud and then talk through some simple questions. *What stands out to you in this chapter? What confuses you? What do we learn about God in this chapter? What questions do you have as we read through it? What do you think we can apply today from what we read?*

6. **Be okay with not having all the answers.** One of the big fears for anyone leading a Bible study is being asked a question and not knowing the answer. It is perfectly okay to not have all the answers. In fact, your teammates will appreciate that about you. When faced with a tough question, just respond by saying "That's a great question, and honestly, I'm not sure how to answer it. Does anybody else want to take a stab at it?" If nobody advances the conversation, assure the individual that you will do some research and get back to them next week.

7. **Be okay with silence.** What if nobody talks? Sometimes, when there is silence, people feel uncomfortable or don't know what to say. Often, however, people just need time to think and process. Silence can be productive. After you ask a question, count to ten slowly in your head as you wait for a response. If nobody responds, ask if it would be helpful if you rephrased the question.

8. **Make one point.** One of the mistakes Bible study leaders make is trying to cram too much material into one study. Think back to the last time you went to church. How much of the sermon do you remember? Probably very little. The Bible study is not your opportunity to knowledge-dump on your unsuspecting teammates. Don't overwhelm them. Find one major theme in the text and keep bringing them back to it.

9. **Be okay with rabbit trails.** Although your goal is to have one main takeaway, be okay with rabbit trails your teammates may want to go down. At the end of the day, the Bible study is for them. If they ask a question that is not relevant to what you are trying to do, feel the freedom to move in that direction. God may be up to something different than what you had planned.

10. **Pray.** Don't neglect this. It may be the most powerful thing that happens at the study. Bookend the Bible study with prayer. As you finish up, ask for prayer requests from your teammates, and then pray for them according to their requests. The following week, ask them about the particular area in their life that you prayed about.

Athlete, God has a purpose for you where you are right now. You bring glory to him when you take faith steps to make an eternal impact.

CHAPTER 14

ON PLATFORM

*Sport has the power to change the world. It has the
power to inspire, it has the power to unite people
in a way that little else does. It speaks to youth in a
language they understand. Sport can create hope,
where once there was only despair.*

—Nelson Mandela

C hristian athletes and fans generally love the concept of
the athletic platform. We love the idea that God has put
certain individuals in the spotlight, and those people can
use their spotlight to talk about Christ. We champion the reality
that sports are a universal language and a cultural megaphone
that we can leverage for God's glory.

To be honest, though, I'm tired of it. Not because I don't
believe in the power of a platform. The mission statement of
the ministry I currently serve reads, "Our mission is to build

spiritual movements everywhere through the platform of sports so that everyone knows someone who truly follows Jesus."[1] So it's part of my job to care about platforms.

I also believe that having a platform is a biblical concept. Remember the story from Acts 14? The crowds were worshipping Paul and Barnabas because they had healed a man. The two men of God immediately deflected the praise lavished on them and sought to get the spotlight off of themselves. We need to finish the story because it doesn't end with them running from the crowd. Everyone is cheering them on and watching their every move. They have a platform. The first thing they do is tell everyone to calm down. They are just men—not gods. This was not false humility but an earnest plea for the crowd to stop directing their praise at them. The last thing they wanted to do was steal any glory due the Lord. After putting a stop to the false worship going on, they started sharing the gospel with the crowd. Listen to how quickly they transition to sharing the good news: "Men, why are you doing these things? We also are men, of like nature with you, and we bring you good news, that you should turn from these vain things to a living God, who made the heaven and the earth and the sea and all that is in them" (Acts 14:15).

No, I have not grown tired of leveraging a platform for God's glory through sharing the gospel with a crowd who is hanging on my every word. What I have grown tired of is how the idea of a platform has become reduced to a shout-out to God after a successful outcome. The athletic platform has come to mean this: People are watching, so make sure you give God credit. Somehow, we have assumed that lives can be transformed as a result of us verbally giving glory to God after a competition. It has become a box-checking exercise for "good" Christian athletes. It's a similar mindset to that of inviting our friends to church and assuming we've done our part, leaving the rest up to the pastor.

Your platform doesn't automatically make you an effective ambassador for Christ. It just means you have people's attention. If Christian athletes want to capitalize on the platform God has so graciously given to them, they need to pick their spots more strategically. A platform to spread God's love is an amazing gift, but it becomes most useful when it is leveraged with the right people in the right circumstances.

We need to clear up one more misconception about athletic platforms, that star athletes are the only athletes who have a platform. They are not. If you are an athlete at any level of skill, you usually have a sphere of influence that surpasses the NARP (non-athletic regular person).

I believe an athlete's platform can especially influence younger teammates, the surrounding community, and social media followers. What follows is an encouragement to leverage your platform to these three groups, as well as practical tips on how to do it appropriately.

Engage Younger Teammates for God's Glory

To this day, I remember walking into the locker room as a freshman at Wake Forest University and having three encounters with seniors on the team in just the first week.

The first guy was Chris. He was the star of the track team. Fast, good looking, extroverted. I will never forget walking into the locker room wearing black warmups, shirtless, two-strapping my backpack, and my hat on backward. As I made my way to my locker, Chris looked at me and said affirmingly, "Smith, I like your style, man." I left practice that day with confidence. I was a skinny little runt, but this senior affirmed something he liked about me.

The second interaction came a few days later after a hard workout. I had developed blisters on the heels of my feet that began to bleed midway through practice. By the end of the afternoon, the backs of my new white training shoes were stained red. Another senior, Ted, approached me as we were making our way toward the ice baths. Ted was not the most talented runner, but he worked his butt off. He was one of the best distance runners in the conference his junior and senior years. "Smith, you're gonna be one of the best to ever graduate from this school." He was way off. I ended up having a pretty awful running career. But more than fifteen years later, I can still recall how much I valued and appreciated that comment.

The third moment came courtesy of Paul, one of the only black runners on the team. Without any warning, he approached me after practice, sized me up, and said, "Smith! Are you a racist?" Very few times in my life have I felt as humiliated and small as I did in that moment. I would learn in the coming weeks that Paul did that with everyone as a way of messing with them. Knowing that didn't make me feel any better. Now, if there were a Hall of Fame for the nicest guys to ever run track at Wake Forest University, Paul would get in on the first ballot. But because of that experience, I was very hesitant for the rest of my freshman year to engage with people who didn't share my skin color.

What's the point of mentioning these interactions? Almost two decades have passed since that time, and I still remember them as if they were yesterday. Young athletes are impressionable. They are looking to follow someone's lead. If you have veteran status on the team—and if you don't now, you will someday—you have a platform you can use to speak words of life or death into the younger athletes on the team. Choose the former.

The Bible tells us that "death and life are in the power of the tongue" (Prov. 18:21). Our words carry a lot of weight. We have the opportunity through our words to be a fountain of life (Prov. 10:11) and a tree of life (Prov. 15:4) and to bring healing to others (Prov. 12:18). Athletes bring glory to God when they go out of their way to speak life into their teammates. You have a platform with the younger people on your team. Take advantage of it.

Look for Ways to Serve in Your Community for God's Glory

As a competitive athlete, you have probably noticed that when you compete, there is often background noise that tends to get louder when you perform better. The background noise is coming from the fans. Unless you have parents who need to settle down a little bit, the bulk of the crowd noise comes from members of the community who are cheering for you or the team you are representing. Those community members are comprised of teachers, parents, church members, alumni, children, and many others. If you think they are excited when your team brings home a win, know that they might be even more excited if you take time out of your schedule to talk to them.

Again, you do not need to be the star athlete on the team to do that. If you wear a jersey, you have a platform. One of the best ways you can leverage your platform as an athlete within your community is to share your testimony with local churches, youth

> *If you wear a jersey, you have a platform.*

groups, or elementary schools. Rarely will these opportunities fall into your lap. They must be sought out. Make it a point at some time in the next three months to contact a local church in the area and say something like this: "My name is Brian, and I am on the cross-country team at Wake Forest University. I have been working on sharing my testimony, and I would love the opportunity to share it in front of the youth group at your church. Is this something you would be interested in and could help coordinate?"

If they say yes, bring a younger teammate with you.

Leverage Your Social Media Platform for God's Glory

As Christian athletes, we can easily fall into the trap of thinking the content that spills out of our social media accounts should be all about us. Christian athletes would be wise to leverage their social media accounts for the glory of God.

A business concept that's gained steam in the lives of individuals over the last few years is the idea of branding yourself. Simply put, this means making sure people see you in a certain light that benefits your long-term prospects and personal brand identity. But for the Christian athlete, promoting yourself should always be a secondary concern. Don't be fooled by the hype. Whatever platform you currently have to influence others is a stewardship granted to you by God. He wants you to learn to use it for his purposes and not merely for your own.

I want to help you think about how to do that more effectively and offer some tracks to run down you may never have considered.

Get Better Simply by Avoiding Stupidity

Most social media resources for athletes revolve around a common theme: Don't be a moron. It makes sense. Former Arkansas Coach Bret Bielema echoes many other coaches' philosophies when he says social media plays a big part in who he recruits. "He's got to have a GPA that I can relate to, an ACT or SAT score or a pre-ACT score, and the third box is for social media," says Bielema.[2]

Coaches pay attention to what their current and future athletes are doing on social media. But you already know that.

J. J. Watt, star defensive end for the Houston Texans, once said, "Read each tweet about 95 times before sending it. Look at every Instagram post about 95 times before you send it. A reputation takes years, and years, and years to build, and it takes one press of a button to ruin. So don't let that happen to you. Just be very smart about it."[3]

Coaches and players alike are learning that social media can be a reflection of an athlete's character. Because this is true, most suggestions for how to use social media fall under the category of helping you not make a fool of yourself. That's not a bad thing.

Like fire, social media has potential to do great harm if we are not careful with it. There is wisdom in exercising great caution when it comes to how it's used. But it is also loaded with positive potential if we know how to use it correctly.

Don't Be Offensive — But Stay on Offense

Athletes have a platform, so it's beneficial to talk through how to use it well, not merely how to avoid using it in ways that hurt you and others. We need a higher standard, especially as followers of Christ, for how to leverage our social media accounts for the glory of God.

> We need a higher standard, especially as followers of Christ, for how to leverage our social media accounts for the glory of God.

I have been on Twitter for a couple of years and have about 200 people following me. Very few people care what I have to say. How many people are following you? These people have chosen to pay attention to what you have to say on a daily basis. What are you feeding them?

Before we dive into the five things you should be doing on your social media accounts, let me point out a couple things about social media.

1. Social media is different from any other media outlets. If you get interviewed after a game and talk about Jesus, people watching, listening, and reading are, in a sense, forced to pay attention to you. It is why most people who are not Christians get annoyed when we talk about our faith. But in the world of social media, people choose to listen to you.

2. Whatever brand identity you are going for, if you identify as a follower of Christ, making him known had better play a big part in that.

Since people are choosing to pay attention to what you have to say, here are five things you should be doing.

Share Edifying Content

You have an incredible opportunity to impact your audience by simply sharing good content with them. This assumes you know where to find it.

What do you regularly read or pay attention to that draws you closer to God? Hopefully, one of those streams you pull from is the Bible. If you can't think of any online source from which you are consistently drawing, here are a few recommendations: desiringgod.org, relevantmagazine.com, athletesinaction.org.

How you share something also matters. Whatever you do, don't just copy and paste a link for your audience to click on. Give it your stamp of approval and make a comment about it. At the same time, understand that the majority of non-Christians consider Christians preachy and hypocritical, so you won't always get the response you'd like. That's okay. Keep sowing seeds.

What you share with your audience and the tone you use matter just as much, if not more. Here are a few creative ways to promote someone else's content in a way that is humble and thought provoking.

"This piece by _____ was super challenging to me. Check it out!"

"I was so convicted after reading this. Take a look and let me know what you think."

"Reading this really changed my perspective on _____. I think you will be challenged too!"

Encourage Your Followers to Follow Pastors, Ministry Leaders, and Sports Ministries

Introduce your followers to people and ministries whose purpose is to provide great content to their followers. For example, here are the digital mission statements of a couple of the ministries I mentioned above:

> Desiring God exists to help people everywhere understand and embrace the truth that God is most glorified in us when we are most satisfied in Him.[4]

> Athletesinaction.org exists to help sports-minded people live and think biblically at the intersection of sports and Christianity.[5]

There are plenty of ministries and individuals out there whose sole mission it is to provide faithful, relevant biblical content from which people can benefit. Is your mission to do something similar?

Probably not. And that's okay.

But God has gifted you with a talent that makes other people pay attention to you. Every once in a while, tell them to pay attention to someone else. Here are a couple of ways to do that:

Twitter: "If you're not following _____ already, I would highly encourage you to. He/she/they have helped me grow so much in my faith!"

Facebook: "If you haven't liked the fan page of _____, do so now. With all of the junk that comes across our newsfeeds, what he/she/they produce will be a refreshing change for you!"

Instagram: "If you are not following _____, you need to start now! Check him/her/them out. You won't regret it!"

Athlete, you are probably excellent at playing whatever sport God has gifted you to play. Pastors, writers, and other ministry leaders are good at connecting with people about spiritual issues because God has gifted them as well. Introduce your audience to people and ministries who specialize in delivering consistently edifying digital content.

Repent Publicly and Privately

Your followers need to know that what separates Christians from everyone else is not moral perfection, but forgiveness. Even more, the forgiveness granted to you was not earned, but given freely (Ephesians 2:8–9). The Bible calls that grace. If you end up cursing out an official, get on social media and apologize to your fans. To some extent at least, they view you as representing Jesus. If your sport is not televised, get on social media and tell your audience what happened. Don't make excuses. Apologize.

I believe some of us also need to repent privately about how we use social media. Most of us have been made aware of the dangers of making sports an idol in our lives. Countless articles, blogs, sermons, and chapels have been created around the idea that we should not derive our identity from what we do on the playing field. But how many of us check our followers on a daily basis and gather a sense of satisfaction from the increasing numbers? How many of us feel a sense of pride as our fan base becomes more enamored with us? Conversely, how many of us feel inadequate in this area? How many of us wish we had thousands of people paying attention to what we have to say? If you find yourself in this category, I encourage you to repent privately to God for social media becoming an idol in your life.

Keep this in mind as well. What makes a Christian a Christian is that they are forgiven, not perfect. When you screw up—and you will—know that the discipline of repenting is glorifying to God.

Be a Real Human

Post images and share about what you do on an everyday basis. Many people put athletes on a pedestal. Your sport gives you an elevated position in our culture. A 2013 study showed that athletes have more influence in our society than pastors.[6] People are listening to you because you are good at sports. If you want to actually influence them, however, you need to show that you are like them. Your followers need to know that you are normal. When they see that you are normal and then you offer a tweet like "Check out this article from _____, it was super helpful for me in my walk with Christ," they are more likely to engage with you and the article.

Ask for Prayer

If you have thousands of people who choose to pay attention to what you have to say, why wouldn't you ask for them to pray for you? As we've said, many fans put athletes on a pedestal. One way to actively push against that is to ask for prayer. When you ask for prayer, you are humbling yourself and saying, "I need help," which is the essence of the gospel.

Encourage people to pray either for you or for things that are important to you—a cultural event, things happening on campus (if you're in college) or in the city where you play, something happening at church, a Tweet or piece of social media, or a news story that caught your attention. Why not lead people to stop talking about you or to you and instead encourage them to speak to God alongside of you?

Seventy-eight percent of Americans are on social media, and a handful of them are paying attention to you. Keep learning how to be a good steward of the talent God has given you and the messages you communicate to the people he has put in place who listen to what you have to say.

CONCLUSION

We don't obey Jesus to get something from Jesus.
We obey because he gave us himself.
We get him. He is the treasure.

—Derwin L. Gray

In the fall of 2007, I did something stupid. I signed up to compete in an Ironman. After watching the race take place in Madison, Wisconsin, I thought, *I could do that.* So I signed up the next day. After a year of training, I toed the line on September 11, 2008, at Ironman Wisconsin, with my sights set on qualifying for the World Championship in Kona. After a 2.4-mile swim, a 112-mile bike ride, and 26.2-mile run, I came up about six places shy of my goal. (It didn't help that my right knee decided to stop working with about 10 miles to go on the run.) The competition took me 10 hours and 25 minutes to complete.

A day after the race, I sat down in front of a computer and typed my summary of the race, detailing every bit of it I could recall. Although I remember a few distinct moments from that day, most of it is a blur. But if I hadn't written that recap, many of the amazing memories from the competition would have been lost.

Maybe you're feeling that way right now. You have read through this entire book. Maybe, hopefully, there were some "aha" moments and practical tips that will help shift the trajectory of how you leverage your sport for God's glory. But perhaps you have forgotten the majority of it. It was a lot of information. So a recap could be helpful. It might make it easier to retain some key points. To this day, my Ironman recap helps me remember the highlights from what was a really crazy day. Hopefully this quick recap can do the same for this book.

Introduction

- The word *glory* has turned into a buzzword we flippantly toss around because it is the right answer. But how many of us know what it means?
- We need to learn and execute on making our sport serve us in a way that draws us closer to God.
- When we use our sport to get more of God, we are aligning ourselves with the way God intended his good gifts, like sports, to work.

Chapter 1: On Glory

- What God desires most is his glory. As John Piper says, "God has many other goals in what he does. But none of them is more ultimate than this."[1]
- Glory simply means weight.
- God's glory is, at least, the weight of everything that makes him God and the going public of that weight for others to notice.
- Giving God glory means thinking and acting in a way that pleases him and draws attention to who he is.

Chapter 2: On God

- God is not indifferent to anything that takes place within his universe, which includes how you play and think about your sport.
- The gospel shows us that God is pleased with us, not because of anything we do or did, but because of what Jesus has already done for us.
- By choosing to give God his due only after our athletic successes, we reinforce the stereotype of God being like a fan, a coach, or an owner who is only interested in wins and losses.
- We must view God through the lens he wants to be viewed through—as our Father.

Chapter 3: On Athletes

- Instead of imaging ourselves to be strong like a lion, we would be wise to think of ourselves as sheep—dumb, directionless, defenseless.
- Having a proper view of ourselves aids in the fight against pride.
- Humility is like a muscle—it gets stronger when pushed. That is, we practice humility, seeking the low place of service rather than self-promotion.

Chapter 4: On Motivation

- We often wrongly believe that Philippians 4:13 means we can achieve any outcome in our sport because of Christ.
- In its proper context, Philippians 4:13 means that we can have contentment regardless of the outcome because of Christ.
- A focal point is something you can quickly concentrate on that realigns your focus on your ultimate motivation in your sport: glorifying God.

Chapter 5: On Winning

- Celebrating good things that happen is not evidence of a lack of humility; it is part of how God designed us to react.
- Winning is great, and we should desire to pursue it, but there is a good reason why it does not satisfy you at a soul level. It was never supposed to.
- Don't relegate giving your best to game-day performances. Don't be habitually lazy in practice, in the weight room, and with your eating and sleeping habits, and then give it 100 percent during competition and claim, "All glory to God!"
- Go ahead and pray for the win.
- Accept praise humbly and graciously.

Chapter 6: On Losing

- It's alright to be frustrated when you lose. You're human. Don't fake a positive emotion to appear godly.
- When a Christian athlete loses and still makes much of Jesus, non-Christians notice and often want to know more from that athlete. Anyone can make much of Jesus after a win.
- Our obedience should be birthed out of a desire to please our heavenly Father, not out of a misguided belief that our goodness can be exchanged for an earthly blessing like athletic success. God is not a genie.

Chapter 7: On Injuries

- Be honest with God about how you are feeling; he can handle it.
- God may be preparing you for something in the future through your current circumstance.
- God may want you to deal with something in the present, and your injury is the pause on which you need to focus.

- You may be injured because God wants to use you to reach someone else.

Chapter 8: On Practice

- For the Christian athlete, practice should primarily be about others, not you.
- Your motivation in practice should be to engage in it as if you were doing it for the Lord.
- Relationships will always have more lasting value and joy than the trophies you earn.
- God has designed our bodies in such a way that when we exercise, we experience increased happiness (endorphins, etc.).

Chapter 9: On Teammates

- Despite unfortunate circumstances, Jonathan chose to act as a faithful friend instead of complaining.
- Great teammates seek to put others above themselves, especially in moments when it is most difficult to do so.
- Great teammates do not lurk behind the scenes looking for an opportunity to capitalize on the misfortune of others.
- Your most significant impact as an athlete may be on the teammates with whom you rub shoulders every day.

Chapter 10: On Gray Areas

- God stared into the face of chaos and created order. What does that look like in sports? Simply put, we follow the rules of the game.
- When we choose to operate with integrity in every way possible, we image our Creator.
- Doing the right thing doesn't mean you'll come out on top of the scoreboard.
- Athletes who take a hard line on gray areas are susceptible to becoming prideful or at least being seen as prideful.

Be aware of what is going on in your heart and aware of how others might see you. Keep in mind that if you follow all the rules, obey the letter of the law, so to speak, and it still creates pride in you, you are sinning. Attitude counts, too.

Chapter 11: On Retirement

- Moving on from your athletic career often involves a grieving process. It can be hard. That's a natural reaction to losing something and should be expected.
- The ups and downs of sports can set a standard of excitement that makes the next stage of your life feel comparatively dull.
- Many of the same things you enjoyed in your sport can be found and experienced through involvement in the local church.

Chapter 12: On Coaches

- It's our job as God's lights in this dark world to submit, smile, and display the life and love of Jesus in harsh and unfair situations.
- You can avoid a lot of disappointment if you release any unrealistic expectations you may have placed on your coach.
- When you show the desire to be a continual learner, you honor your coach as the teacher—and glorify God.
- Christian athletes are called to stand out from the crowd, to look different. Resist the urge to gossip about your coach.

Chapter 13: On Mission

- To be an effective spiritual leader on your team, you need to learn how to articulate the gospel and how to put your story into words.
- The best way to change the culture on your team is to create a new culture.

- A team Bible study can be one of the most effective ways you can create a new culture on your team.

Chapter 14: On Platform

- Your platform does not automatically make you an effective ambassador for Christ. It just means you have people's attention.
- If you have veteran status on the team—and if you don't now, you will someday—you have a platform to speak words of life into younger athletes on the team.
- Opportunities to leverage your platform will rarely fall into your lap. You must seek them out.
- Use your social media to strategically engage your followers. Remember, they chose to follow you, so don't be afraid to be bold.

There is one last thing I want to remind you of before the close of this book. Do you remember our discussion about Paul and Barnabas in Acts 14 and how their story provides a model for the modern-day Christian athlete to follow? Let's briefly review what happened.

- They do something amazing (heal a man).
- The crowds around them go crazy, worshipping the two men as if they were gods.
- They respond in humility by saying they are not gods, just normal guys like everyone else.
- But now they have a platform. People are paying attention to what they're saying. They know the gospel well and use this opportunity to share with the crowd about the one true God.
- What else could God ask of these two? They are intentional, skillful, humble, and opportunistic. Surely, God will bless their efforts, right? Let's see.
- "Even with these words they scarcely restrained the people from offering sacrifice to them. But Jews came

from Antioch and Iconium, and having persuaded the crowds, they stoned Paul and dragged him out of the city, supposing that he was dead" (Acts 14:18–19).

Are You Kidding Me?

They did everything God could ask of them, yet somehow the crowds turned on them, and Paul was stoned to the point that he appeared to be dead. Well, he wasn't. And when he finally came to, what do you think he did? What would *you* do in that situation?

> But when the disciples gathered about him, he rose up and entered the city, and on the next day he went on with Barnabas to Derbe. When they had preached the gospel to that city and had made many disciples, they returned to Lystra and to Iconium and to Antioch, strengthening the souls of the disciples, encouraging them to continue in the faith, and saying that through many tribulations we must enter the kingdom of God (Acts 14:20–22).

Athlete, let this story and others like it in the Bible serve to teach you a fundamental truth: Our obedience to God does not mean that things will always play out as we expect or would like. My hope is that you put into practice as many things in this book as possible, but please, please, do not think that just because you begin to give glory to God through your sport that he is now obligated to grant you athletic success in return. He might. But he might not. Your obedience and willingness to glorify him should not come with strings attached. Struggles and hardships will come. They always do. Be ready for them.

Our obedience to God does not mean that things will always play out as we expect or would like.

My prayer for you is that your response to adversity will be similar to Paul's and that you will persevere when things get tough. My prayer is that when you fall, you will get back up, surrounded by a community to help you tend to your wounds and get back into the game, trusting that God will sustain you as you seek to give him the glory due his name through your sport and through your life.

Thank you for reading *The Assist*! I pray that this book has blessed and informed you and given you some firm takeaways as you serve God in sports.

If you would like a free study guide to use in small groups, you can download *The Assist Study Guide* for FREE at theassistbook.com.

ACKNOWLEDGMENTS

To Lucid Books: Thank you for believing in this project enough to partner with me in it.

To my editor, Matt Erickson: Thanks for hammering through the manuscript, making it better, and dealing with my constant barrage of texts asking for an update.

To all the financial and prayer supporters of our ministry with Athletes in Action: We promised you when we joined the staff that we would do more than sit in coffee shops all day. (Confession: I spent a lot of time in coffee shops working on this. Hopefully, the end will justify the means.) Thank you for your partnership in the gospel with Linsey and me. This book is a result of your investment in us.

To Ed Uszynski: Much of what is written in this book is a result of your helping mold the clay of my imaginative wheel.

To Hudson, Hadassah, and Judah: each of you is beautiful, unique, and loved.

To Linsey: You are—and always will be—my best friend and the love of my life. This book didn't happen without your affirmation of me as a man, a writer, and a minister of the gospel. You gave me confidence and freedom (and time away from the house projects) to see this book to the finish line.

NOTES

Chapter 1

1. John Piper, *Desiring God: Meditations of a Christian Hedonist* (Sisters, OR: Multnomah Press, 1986), 42–43.

2. This glory verses list was adapted from John Piper, "Biblical Texts to Show God's Zeal for His Own Glory," *Desiring God*, November 24, 2007, https://www.desiringgod.org/articles/biblical-texts-to-show-gods-zeal-for-his-own-glory.

3. Defining glory idea taken from John Piper, "What Is God's Glory?" *Desiring God*, July 22, 2014, https://www.desiringgod.org/interviews/what-is-god-s-glory.

4. Timothy Keller, @timkellernyc, *Twitter.com*, August 13, 2014, https://twitter.com/timkellernyc/status/499691880540823552.

5. Piper, "What is God's Glory?"

Chapter 2

1. Dr. Ed Uszynski, "How to Respond to the 'God Doesn't Care Who Wins' Critic," *Athletes in Action*, April 2, 2017, https://athletesinaction.org/underreview/does-god-care-that-the-patriots-won.

2. Richard J. Mouw, *Abraham Kuyper: A Short and Personal Introduction* (Grand Rapids: Eerdmans, 2011), 4.

3. Timothy Keller, *The Prodigal God: Recovering the Heart of the Christian Faith* (New York: Riverhead Books, 2008), 45.

4. J. I. Packer, *Knowing God* (Downers Grove, IL: InterVarsity Press, 1973), 200.

5. Ibid., 201.

6. Charles R. Swindoll, *Growing Strong in the Seasons of Life* (Grand Rapids, MI: Zondervan, 1994), 61.

Chapter 3

1. Piper, *Desiring God: Meditations of a Christian Hedonist*, 250.

2. Idea from: Passion City Church, "The Good Shepherd" (Podcast), September 18, 2016, http://passioncitychurch. libsyn.com/the-good-shepherd.

3. Tim Challies, "Dumb, Directionless, Defenseless," *Challies.com*, August 26, 2013, *https://www.challies.com/christian-living/dumb-directionless-defenseless/*.

4. Max Lucado, *Lucado 3-in-1: Traveling Light, Next Door Savior, Come Thirsty* (Nashville: Thomas Nelson, 2008), Google Books.

5. Challies, "Dumb, Directionless, Defenseless."

6. Verses taken from Kevin Black, "The Truth That Helped Helen Maroulis Transcend Gold," *Athletes in Action*, December 26, 2016, https://athletesinaction.org/underreview/the-truth-that-helped-helen-hmaroulis-transcend-gold#. WYypgcbMz-Z.

7. Robert Coram, *Boyd: The Fighter Pilot Who Changed the Art of War* (New York: Little, Brown and Company, 2002), 319.

Chapter 4

1. C. S. Lewis, *The Weight of Glory* (New York: HarperCollins, 1980), 26.

2. Kurt Earl, "Focus: Finding Your Focal Point," Compete4Christ, January 22, 2016, http://compete4christ. co/2016/01/22/focus/.

3. Black, "The Truth That Helped Helen Maroulis Transcend Gold."

4. Wes Neal, *The Handbook on Athletic Perfection* (Grand Island, NE: Cross Training Publishing, 2003), 132.

Chapter 5

1. C. S. Lewis, *Reflections on the Psalms* (New York: Harcourt, Brace and World, 1958), 95.

2. Daniel Schorn, "Tom Brady: The Winner," *60 Minutes*, November 3, 20015, http://www.cbsnews.com/news/tom-brady-the-winner/3/.

3. Herbert McCabe, *God, Christ, and Us* (London: Continuum Publishing, used by permission of Bloomsbury Publishing Plc, 2005), 105.

4. Sam Crabtree, *Practicing Affirmation* (Wheaton, IL: Crossway, 2011), 127–128.

Chapter 6

1. J. R. R. Tolkien, *The Fellowship of the Ring* (London: Allen and Unwin, 1954), 294.

2. Stephen Altrogge, *Game Day for the Glory of God: A Guide for Athletes, Fans, and Wannabes* (Wheaton, IL: Crossway, 2008), 79–81.

3. Ibid., 93.

4. Don Pearson and Paul Santhouse, *Youth Work—Let God Use Your Influence: 99 Practical Ideas for Youthworkers, Parents & Volunteers* (Chicago: Moody Publishers, 2009), 33–34.

5. Dr. Seuss, *AZ Quotes*, http://www.azquotes.com/quote/922897.

Chapter 7

1. Dr. Henry Cloud, *Changes That Heal* (Grand Rapids, MI: Zondervan, 1992), 25.

2. Kaitlin Miller, "Don't Resent God's Training Ground," *Desiring God*, January 31, 2017, http://www.desiringgod.org/articles/don-t-resent-god-s-training-ground.

3. Matt Chandler, "Of Danger and Ditches," *The Village Church Resources*, March 15, 2008, https://www.tvcresources.net/resource-library/sermons/of-danger-and-ditches.

Chapter 8

1. Leo Widrich, "What Happens to Our Brains When We Exercise and How It Makes Us Happier," *Blog.bufferapp.com*, August 23, 2012, https://blog.bufferapp.com/why-exercising-makes-us-happier.

2. M. K. McGovern, "The Effects of Exercise on the Brain," *serendip.brynmawr.edu*, July 19, 2012, http://serendip.brynmawr.edu/bb/neuro/neuro05/web2/mmcgovern.html.

3. John Piper, *When I Don't Desire God: How to Fight for Joy* (Wheaton, IL: Crossway, 2013), 203.

Chapter 10

1. Jeff Bradley, "Brian Davis Taught Us Integrity, Honesty," *ESPN*, April 19, 2011, http://www.espn.com/golf/columns/story?id=6375777&columnist=bradley_jeff.

2. Ibid.

3. "Grey Area," *Cambridge English Dictionary Online*, https://dictionary.cambridge.org/us/dictionary/english/grey-area.

4. Uszynski, "Your Call?" *Athletes in Action*, January 25, 2016, https://athletesinaction.org/your-call#.WYzlRcbMyt8.

Chapter 11

1. Prim Siripipat, "Moving on from Sports: A College Athlete's Greatest Challenge," *ESPN*, April 11, 2016, http://www.espn.com/espnw/voices/article/15182997/moving-sports-college-athlete-greatest-challenge.

2. Dr. Henry Cloud and Dr. John Townsend, *How People Grow: What the Bible Reveals about Personal Growth* (Grand Rapids, MI: Zondervan, 2001), 135.

3. Emma Vickers, "Life after Sport: Depression in the Retired Athlete," *believeperform.com*, n.d., http://believeperform. com/wellbeing/life-after-sport-depression-in-retired-athletes/.

4. Peter Crutchley, "Why Do So Many Athletes Struggle to Cope with Retirement?" *BBC Sport*, December 18, 2012, http://beta.bbc.com/sport/0/20646102.

5. Uszynski, "The 5 Reasons Athletes Can't Retire," *Athletes in Action*, March 24, 2017, https://athletesinaction.org/underreview/the-5-reasons-athletes-cant-retire#. WYzo58bMyt9.

6. Ibid.

7. Matt Perman. *What's Best Next: How the Gospel Transforms the Way You Get Things Done* (Grand Rapids, MI: Zondervan, 2014), 193.

8. Monica A. Frank, "Issues When Ending a Sports Career," *Excel at Life*, n.d., https://www.excelatlife.com/articles/ending_career.htm.

9. Cloud and Townsend, 136.

10. Francis Chan, *Multiply: Disciples Making Disciples* (Colorado Springs: David C. Cook, 2012), 52.

11. John Piper, *Brothers, We Are Not Professionals: A Plea to Pastors for Radical Ministry* (Nashville: B&H Publishing Group, 2013), 219.

12. J. Campbell White, quoted in John Piper, "There Is No Greater Satisfaction: God-Centered Motivation for World Missions," *Desiring God*, October 1, 1990, https://www.desiringgod.org/articles/there-is-no-greater-satisfaction.

Chapter 12

1. Madison Trout, "The Coach That Killed My Passion: An open letter to the coach that made me hate a sport I once loved," *Odyssey*, August 15, 2016, https://www.theodysseyonline.com/to-the-coach-that-killed-my-passion.

2. Matthew C. Mitchell, *Resisting Gossip: Winning the War of the Wagging Tongue* (Fort Washington, PA: CLC Publications, 2013), 23.

3. Trout.

Chapter 14

1. "About," *Athletes in Action*, https://goaia.org/about#vision.

2. "Bad Behavior on Social Media Can Cost Student Athletes," *CBS News*, August 11, 2014, https://www.cbsnews.com/news/bad-behavior-on-social-media-can-cost-student-athletes/.

3. Doug Samuels, "JJ Watt Shares Some Social Media Advice for High School Athletes," *Football Scoop*, July 17, 2015, http://footballscoop.com/news/jj-watt-has-some-social-media-advice-for-high-school-athletes/.

4. John Piper, "The Story of Ian & Larissa," *Desiring God*, May 8, 2012, https://www.desiringgod.org/articles/the-story-of-ian-larissa.

5. Brian Smith, "The Christian Athlete's Guide to Social Media," *Athletes in Action*, October 10, 2016, https://athletesinaction.org/underreview/christian-athletes-guide-to-social-media#.WiK6ZlWnHIU.

6. "Athletes Influence Greater Than Faith Leaders," *Barna*, April 10, 2013, https://www.barna.com/research/athletes-influence-greater-than-faith-leaders/.

Conclusion

1. Piper, *Desiring God*, 42.

CPSIA information can be obtained
at www.ICGtesting.com
Printed in the USA
FFHW011021171019
55613480-61431FF

9 781632 961815